# 63 Alfred Street:
## *Where Capitalism Failed*

The Life and Times of a Venetian Gothic
Mansion in Downtown Detroit

Cover Design: John Kossik
Front Cover Picture: Turret of Ransom Gillis House, July 2004,
© John Kossik
Back Cover Pictures: Ransom Gillis House, February 2005, © John Kossik;
Ransom Gillis House (c. 1876), Courtesy of the Burton Historical Collection,
Detroit Public Library
Find out more at www.63alfred.com

*To*
*My Parents, for teaching me Right from Wrong*
*My Teachers, for teaching me of Reading, Writing, Arithmetic, and Revolution*
*My Children, for teaching me Patience*
*And*
*To my Wife Carolyn, without whom I would be hopelessly lost*

*The view which he has given of human life has a melancholy hue, but he feels conscious that he has drawn these dark tints from a conviction that they are really in the picture, and not from a jaundiced eye or an inherent spleen of disposition.*

*-Thomas Malthus, An Essay on the Principle of Population, 1798*

## Acknowledgements

Many, many people have helped me in developing this book since I unknowingly happened upon the house on one of my annual pilgrimages back home to Detroit in the Summer of 2004. I will try to note them all below, please excuse me if I miss someone.

After my family I would first and foremost like to thank my long-time friend and Wheelman Andy Crause. I would also like to thank, in alphabetical order; Ed Allotta, Louise Barker (Family Archivist, Society of the Descendants of Norman Fox), Peter Binno (Essa's), Helen Broughton, Dr. Thomas W. Brunk, Catherine Cangany (Relative of Henry T. Brush), Pete Essa (John and Amina Essa's Nephew), Rob Goodspeed, Bruce Harkness, Sherry Huntington (Downriver Historical Society), Brian Hurttienne (BVH Architecture, Inc.), David Jones (Williamston Historical Society), Gerri Kelley (Pewabic Pottery), Kristine Kidorf (Kidorf Preservation Consulting), Donald King (Great Grandson of Henry T. Brush), Glen King (Relative of Henry T. Brush), Mike Kirk, Douglas Kuykendall (63 Alfred's last owner), Kristy Lambe, Fran LaMont, Vonciel LeDuc (Manistique historical society), Jim Marusich (City of Detroit), Linda Moore (Hillsdale College), Paul Olsen (Manistique Pioneer-Tribune), Andrew Prevost, Frank Rashid (Marygrove College), Jim Sokol, Del Taft (Grandson of Bert Brush), Eric Taylor (Museum of Snohomish County History), Marilyn VanDyke (Town of Queensbury, NY), Scott Weir (ERA Architects Inc.), Randy Wilcox, and Robert Wright.

John Kossik
February 2010

# Detroit

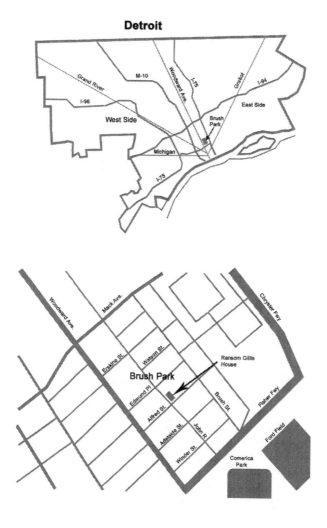

# Contents

# Ruins

*"Man ... you know how many abandoned buildins' we have in Detroit?*
*I mean, how you suppossa take pride in your neighborhood, wit shit like dat next*
*door? And does the City tear 'em down?*
*No, day too busy buildin' casinos and taken money from da people."*
*"Shut your preachin' ass up, nobody care about dat shit."*
*-- Movie, 8 Mile, 2002[1]*

My old college buddy Andy, myself, and my 12-year old son Christopher left the Downriver suburbs of Detroit en route to an area called Brush Park, just across Interstate 75 from the fresh new multimillion-dollar stadiums of Ford Field ----home of the Detroit Lions--- and Comerica Park --- home of the Detroit Tigers. We had ventured there on a hot summer morning in 2004 with a desire to "go find some ruins," ignorant of the unique microcosm of human civilization we were about to stumble upon.

As we traveled up John R, approaching Alfred Street, the ruined presence of a once magnificent structure came into view. It was strikingly comfortable amidst the landscape of vacant and neglected land that allowed an unbroken expanse of pale blue sky to dominate the scene. We parked on John R along side this building. When I opened the car door, the smell of urine was noticeably present. To the north, further up John R, a spattering of other stately brick ruins were present. About 50 yards off, in what seemed to once have been a courtyard, a black man sat hunched over on a bench. A thin white man in his 40's, cigarette in hand, came walking up John R with a small dog in tow. His disheveled "bed head" hair matched that of his dog's. Except for these once elaborate structures, this landscape matched that found in many of Detroit's neighbor-

1

hoods. As my friend Andy was fond of noting, "Hell, it looks like a scene out' a 'Blade Runner.'"[2]

Our attention returned to the house. It's lonely, faded grandeur filled you with a troubling desire to sit down and beg for an autobiography. As we drew closer, the specific details of its architecture and current condition became vividly apparent. This only intensified our curiosity. The structure stood there quietly, fully aware, yet silent, of all that had happened in the area over the last century. Most of the houses left standing in Brush Park were also at one time elegant Victorian beauties, but this one was unique. Maybe this was due to the lack of other structures in close proximity, they had long been demolished in an effort to limit the availability of free accommodations for local crack dealers. Maybe it was the vivid green wild foliage, which engulfed the house, contrasting the red brick of the structure that made it stand out.[3]

No, the turret, the turret - that surely was the thing! It hung there from the front left hand corner of the building, somewhat precariously, with its top portion pulling away from the structure. We anticipated it falling right in front of us while we stood there, as it was held in place only by brick mortar and a makeshift rusted steel post. The post was tucked under the base of the turret as you would under the end of a tent canopy. As we moved closer the turret's details came to light. Contrasting beautifully with the turret's red brick were five rows of tile work that surrounded its equator, four of which were still predominantly intact. The geometric designs of bright blue, red, yellow, and brown hues had held their colors remarkably well through the years. You would have thought they were relatively new if not for the context in which they existed. Below this tile work was a highly ornamental stone base, which narrowed down to an area where, presumably, a pedestal was once present. This pedestal was now replaced by the rusted steel pipe. The windows of the turret, glass probably gone 40 years ago, had their frames tilted and grey, unprotected for decades from the seasonal extremes of southeastern Michigan. In the center turret window, like a small child just tall enough to peek out over the sill, grew a bright green fern.

Andy and I returned to the house on an overcast February day a few months later. The lush green foliage was gone replaced by a few inches of snow that blanketed the surrounding ground as well as any surface of the structure where which it could grab hold. The removal of any suggestion of life only served to accentuate the building's dominance of the scene. As we stood there in the cold just a few steps from the corner an elegant, jet black, BMW 323Ci screamed up John R from the direction of Comerica Park. Seeing us, the car stopped, the passenger window lowered, and the driver, an attractive young black woman dressed in a trim, dark business suit, leaned over and asked, "Do you know the address of this house?" Having been there before we replied, "205 Alfred Street." Her cell phone immediately returned to her ear, the window slowly rose, and she was off as quickly as she had arrived. Years later I found myself watching the movie *Four Brothers* and there right before me was a cameo of the house for about 10 seconds near the end of the film. I could not help but wonder if the young woman we met that day was scouting the area for a desolate clip to reinforce the overall feeling of the film. (released in August of 2005 and set in Detroit, the film was actually shot predominantly in Toronto, Canada)[4]

What series of events could have possibly brought this structure to its current state? Little did I know at the time that this tickle of curiosity would evolve into an overwhelming obsession.

There is something magical about old buildings. You touch them and seem to feel a direct attachment to those long since dead. They had touched the same stone, brick, and tile. At the start of the Iraq war about a year prior to our visit to this house, I remember seeing a picture of US soldiers in front of the Ziggurat of Ur. What an experience! To actually touch something that had been built over 4000 years ago! Were there some long lost "secrets" hidden in there, some "wisdom of the elders" that we had somehow lost over the years? Maybe nothing of modern monetary worth remained at Ur, but there was still knowledge to be uncovered. Of value yes, even if it had only to say that "the more things change, the more they stay the same." Not everyone viewed these old structures with such reverence though. There were media reports that graffiti like 'SEMPER FE' had been spray-painted on this temple when the US military passed through the area.[5]

Americans, due to our recent colonization of the Western Hemisphere, do not have a wealth of old structures to draw insight from. The ones available in the United States, whose origins are from European culture, are just a few hundred years old, a blink of the eye in historical terms. Even though, their history can still invoke in us a guttural response. Such was what we felt as we stood in front of the ruin at the corner of John R and Alfred Street in downtown Detroit on that hot July morning. What had happened through the years to bring this structure to its present state? I found myself feeling as if I were looking at the ruins of Angkor Wat in Cambodia or Machu Picchu in Peru. Westerners have for years romanticized about the histories behind these sites, hoping again that they held some treasured secrets for us. I started wondering if the structure we found in Brush Park could hold the same type of rewards.

The reasons why others were left pondering, and romanticizing, about the lost histories of places like Angkor

Wat and Machu Picchu were not that much different from those we felt about this house in Detroit. The changes that resulted in this lonely ruin probably occurred slowly, due to a complex series of events and how the local people reacted to them. To those present at the time, these changes may have been imperceptible. It was only after a long period of time, when those who unknowingly lived through these events were gone, that others "discovered" what was never really lost and became curious as to the mechanisms that caused this transition.

When Westerners "discovered" the ruins at Machu Picchu, they were abandoned. No one was living amongst what took those before them tremendous effort and sacrifice to create. At other similar sites Westerners found remnant populations, descendants of the original creators, unfortunately, all these descendants knew of their fore-father's greatness had been reduced to myth or melded symbolically into cultural and religious beliefs. This was what had happened in Brush Park. It was still occupied, but was a mere shadow of what it once was. Only rumor and seemingly disassociated facts remained. Unlike the situations present at typical romanticized archaeological ruins though there was a distinct advantage in Detroit. The records of what occurred were less then 140 years old. They were not documented in some abandoned, archaic language, which would take years of study and a "Rosetta Stone" to translate. They were all written in English from a period so close to our present time that their meaning could be easily understood. In addition, these events occurred during a period of time when a large number of the city's inhabitants were literate and newspapers, books, and government records were abundant. This provided the interested investigator far more information then just the names of Kings and the outcomes of battles.

Over the last 150 years, Detroit experienced phe-
nomenal changes, rising to the pinnacle of industrial and
economic strength, and then plunging into deep decay. The
resulting remnant population had then become some of the
poorest and most violent in the nation. The result was a city
with a social and political landscape similar to that in
Europe after the fall of Rome. When Rome fell what was
left of the Empire fell back to their only defensible position,
behind the walls of Byzantium. In their absence a new order formed outside. The vacuum of Rome's demise forced
the indigenous European tribes to fill the void. When the
structure provided by Rome was lost, the remaining population's priorities turned to survival. Roman education, customs, engineering, literature, mathematics, architecture,
were all unwarranted luxuries in this new state of circum-
stances. So steep was this decline that the next Holy Roman
Emperor, Charlemagne, was illiterate.[6] These conditions
facilitated "The Forgetting" that resulted in the marveling,
some two millennia later, at structures that had been there
all the time. There was a significant difference in the case of
Detroit though. Whereas what was left of the Roman culture was protecting itself from the outside world, in Southeastern Michigan the outside world (burgeoning suburbia)
was protecting itself from what was left of Detroit.

As the City of Detroit was slowly abandoned (for
reasons illustrated later in this book) it's social, political,
and economic structure changed dramatically. Those left
behind in the City had no immediate need of the history left
around them. Their time was filled with acquiring the ba-
sics of human survival. After WWII, as Western Europe
and Japan rebuilt their societies, they were forced to choose
foundations on a much more communal and socialistic basis
than in the United States. Why? Because they had "no place
else to go." After two millennia they had filled up their living space and thus needed to learn how to coexist. To the

detriment of cities like Detroit and areas like Brush Park, this was not the case in the United States. When European's arrived on this continent they were presented with a unique and unprecedented situation. What stood before them was a large, fertile, resource-rich land mass, basically free of an indigenous population. The indigenous population of the Americas had been physically separated from the peoples (and microbes) of Europe, Asia, and Africa for as much as 30,000 years. They were tragically susceptible to diseases these "Old World" visitors brought with them. The resulting devastation brought on by these "Old World" diseases claimed as much as 95% of the Native American population.[7] Imagine Steven King's *The Stand*.[8]

This provided the newly arrived European-American's a unique situation. They could freely and easily move to equally life sustaining lands further west once they had "used up" the resources in their current location, all of this while maintaining their culture intact. They paid very little to no price for any prior abandonments. The land to them seemed truly "endless." In reality though they were just repopulating an area that had been wiped clean of its indigenous population. The little these Europeans knew of the potent weapon they brought with them, they attributed to "the good hand of God ... sweeping away great multitudes of natives ... that he might make room for us."[9]

The availability of this free and unoccupied land and the new government's intent on "filling it," proved the true death knell for cities like Detroit, not to mention the unfortunate residents left behind "with no place left to go."

But only facts can convince the reader of the above ideas, and that's what we will explore as we look deeper into the history of this house we found on that bright July morning. Weeks after our visit, upon returning to my home in Seattle, I started looking through all the pictures I had taken on our trip to Brush Park. I found that I had accidentally photographed the address of this iconic structure, spray painted in yellow on the lower right hand corner opposite the turret. It read, 205. Two-O-Five Alfred Street, Hmm ... let's "Google" it. This house was in Brush Park, how about that? Googling "Brush Park," the third result was "The Brush Park Ruins. The Ransom Gillis House at the corner of Alfred and John R. bespeaks the glories of the Gilded Age in Detroit."[10] Googling "Ransom Gillis Home" gave the following information:

> Ransom Gyllis (sp.) Home
> The northwest corner of Alfred at John R in Detroit's Brush Park, one block east of Woodward near downtown Detroit
> Architects; Henry T. Brush and George D. Mason
> Architectural style: Flamboyant and eclectic variations on a Victorian theme
> Date of Completion: 1876
> Use in 2003: Abandoned ruin
> City of Detroit: Local Historic District: Brush Park District. [11]

Subsequently, from the Detroit Historical Designation Advisory Board records:

> 205 Alfred, 1876, Brush & Mason, architects. This house at the corner of John R. and Alfred may have introduced to Detroit the so-called "Venetian Gothic", a style brought to popularity by the The Stones of Venice, an extraordinarily influential book on Venetian art and architecture by John Ruskin, the important English art critic whos work ties in as well with the Pre-Raphaelite movement and the Arts and Crafts movement.

*Ransom Gillis House, Brush & Mason, Architects. This former dwelling is two stories with an irregular footprint. Orange-red common brick was accented with exceptional stone and tile detailing throughout. A third story/mansard roof (completely gone) was covered with gray slate with wrought iron cresting. The remnant of a corner turret with steep conical roof is barely attached. A single story storefront addition was added to the south-west corner but is partially demolished. One highly ornamental chimney that formed the gable end of the roof remains standing on the West side elevation. The gable front on the facade is still standing. Sadly the building has lost integrity due to its poor condition and loss of materials as a result of vandalism and neglect. Pewabic Pottery's first home, this property's coach house, is no longer extant.* [12]

Hmm ... the Ransom Gillis House on the corner of John R and Alfred Street in downtown Detroit. Subsequent investigation found that the address of this house was originally 63 Alfred Street being changed when the City renumbered the streets in the 1920's. But we are getting ahead of ourselves. The true treasure being buried in the details, it was time to start digging. Our story starts with the architect of the Ransom Gillis House at 63/205 Alfred Street, Henry T. Brush.

# Henry T. Brush

*"Mr. Brush was one of the most promising of the younger architects of Detroit, and was without doubt a real artist in his profession."*
                                        *--The Evening News, Detroit*
                                        *July 15, 1879, 4 o'clock Edition*[1]

On August 9th 1849, Henry T. Brush was brought into this world by Amanda Hunter Brush. Amanda was from Michigan, while Henry's Father was from Canada. As this newborn lay in his cradle, no doubt the most interested party in the household was his 3-year-old brother James. The world into which Henry and James were born was one filled with the quickly expanding wonders produced by man's manipulation of science and mathematics. Detroit, the city in which they lived, was at the time positioned to fully exploit these changes.[2]

By the time Henry was 11 his father was gone. Along with his mother and brother, they lived at 32 Montcalm in Detroit, under the watchful eye of William Cicero Grant, who Amanda had recently married. William was essential to the boys' exposure to the beautiful dance of mathematics, science, and art, which was blossoming at the time. William Cicero Grant was a Mathematical Instrument Maker. Mathematical Instrument Makers produced devices such as surveying instruments, barometers, simple Calipers, and countless other items. They fashioned these devices not only to be functional and accurate, but also to be pleasing to the eye. Made of polished, articulate, brass metalwork and rich grained hardwoods, what remains of these devices now rest on museum shelves, the skilled hands that created them long since returned to the earth. William apprenticed this trade while in his mid-30's at the Detroit Firm of Burt & Bailey.  This was the company of William Austin Burt, the inventor of the solar compass as well as the typographer (first American typewriter).  With today's easily accessible handheld computers and GPS devices, most practitioners of the art of surveying have never heard of, let alone seen, a solar compass.  In the 1830's though this tool was essential for European's expansion into the area now called the Upper Peninsula of Michigan.  Burt had invented this tool to assist him in surveying these parts, as it was immune to the affects of the local iron deposits that made a traditional magnetic compass useless.  Burt's Solar Compass used the sighting of the sun to determine the "true meridian" or "true north."  This was a modern extrapolation of Obelisks used by the ancient Egyptians.  Then they measured the distances between the shadows cast by these monuments at different times of the day, ---the "Stride of Ra" as mentioned in ancient texts --- to determine "true north."[3,4,5]

By the time Henry, James, and Amanda lived with Mr. Grant, he was a partner in the Mathematical Instrument Maker firm of Grant & Crosman.  In 1858 "Grant & Crosman ... purchased the establishment of Burt & Watson (formally Burt & Bailey), ... for manufacturing Burt's Solar Compass and Mathematical Instruments generally."  One meticulously crafted, polished brass, Burt's Solar Compass, bearing the Grant & Crosman name, can be found today tucked away in the Museum of Surveying in Lansing, Michigan.[6,7]

Henry and James must have visited William's shop routinely, maybe even worked there in their teens.  They both must have marveled at the combination of science, mathematics, and craftsmanship used to create these magically beautiful tools.  By exposing them to this, William was invaluable in shaping the boy's futures.  Both eventually chose professions in which they used this knowledge to express their own individual creativity.  Henry became an architect, while James became a photographer. Interestingly, the only remaining portrait of Henry in adulthood was the work of his brother James.[8,9,10]

Henry and James were in their teens during the Civil War. Although Detroit had played a critical roll in the Underground Railroad for years prior to the war, its general working-class White population still practiced widespread discrimination against Blacks. "In 1863, following the issuance of the Emancipation Proclamation and the initiation of a national draft, riots broke out in a number of cities in the North, including Detroit."[11] Henry was only 13 when the Detroit Race Riot broke out just 15 blocks from his home on Montcalm. Surely, Henry had read the reports in the city papers of whites heading down Beaubien Street from the jail, axes, spades, rocks, clubs, and bricks in hand, intent on taking out their pent-up anger on the "coloreds" who ran successful cooper shops on Lafayette Street. Such was their fervor that "clubs, brick, and missiles of every description flew like hail," at the defenseless victims. The "official" reason for the riot was the charged "outrages" committed upon a white woman by a black man, but residents of the time knew that the true cause was the deep hatred and jealousy held by many white immigrants against the black population in Detroit. In reality the "outrages" were on two teenage girls, one white and one black whom turned out to be prostitutes. Although William Faulkner who was accused of this crime was assumed to be black his race was actually somewhat nebulous as many of the blood-lines in Detroit had been a mixture of European, American-Indian, and Black since the French first settled it in the 1700's. The anger against Blacks in the City was based in the enclaves of the new white immigrants, Irish and German, who came to Detroit to escape the dire economic conditions in their home countries. These immigrants poor, unskilled, many times illiterate, were angry at the fact that the rich of the city

13

could buy their way out of the current draft and, as would occur time and time again in the following years, took their frustrations out on Blacks. It did not help matters that many of the Blacks in Detroit were skilled workers and thus economically much better off than these new White arrivals.[12] At times it seemed that these feelings of hatred from White immigrants in Detroit exceeded those of Southern Whites.[13]

Perhaps, if the wind was right, Henry and James smelt the smoke that poured from the homes of these unfortunate coopers. Maybe they even had the opportunity to later read the words of one who lived through that demonic night:

> *Strange as it may be, yet 'tis true without doubt,*
> *Mobs do not discriminate if once let out;*
> *So when they had fired the huts of the poor,*
> *They ran with the torch to their rich neighbor's door.*
> *This brought the community plainly to see*
> *The danger in which all were likely to be;*
> *The rich and the poor, the black and the white,*
> *Stood a chance to be mobbed and burned out that night.*
> *I blush when I think that such deeds should take place,*
> *Not heathens or Turks, a civilized race,*
> *Not where savage nations alone have the rule,*
> *But here amidst churches, the Bible and school.*
> *Humanity wept, she lamented the sight,*
> *The groans, blood and tears of that terrible night;*
> *Yet, oh, may the town of Detroit never see*
> *Such a day as the sixth of March, sixty-three.*[14,a]

---

a Little did the author know that this scene would actually repeat itself numerous times over the next 140 years.

By 1868 while still living at home Henry, 18, worked as an architect/draughtsman in Detroit. James had already moved out three years earlier and was establishing himself as a photographer on Jefferson Avenue. Though Henry seemingly had little to no "formal" architectural education, this was not a handicap; most certainly William had prepared them both quite well. In 1872 Henry obtained a job at the Detroit architect office of J.V. Smith & Co. That same year, he married Jeanie Flora Campbell. Henry was 23 and Jeanie was 19. The next year he moved to the firm of Porter & Watkins for a short time before he and Hugh Smith formed their own company. By this time, James was married with an 8-year-old son Edward. Henry's mother, Amanda, never shared these experiences with her sons. She died on March 12th, 1870, just two months shy of her 49th birthday.[15,16,17,18,19,20,21,22,23,24]

Henry's first structure was the Methodist Church of Canada in Chatham, Ontario built in 1873. The church still stands today, but with no "official" mention of Henry attached to it. His next structure was the Orchard Lake Chapel in Orchard Lake, Michigan that has been in continuous use from the time it was built in 1874. The Orchard Lake Chapel was funded by donations from Colin & Caroline Campbell, Jeanie's parents. Eighteen Seventy-four also saw Brush & Smith awarded their first expansive project, the Central Hall at Hillsdale College. With a construction cost of $125,000, it also is still in use today.[25,26,27,28,29,30,31,32]

Even with the onset of the Economic Depression of 1873, Henry's career took off, as did his family. In August of 1874, Jeanie gave birth to their first and only child, Annie Frances. Tragically, Jeanie soon succumbed to complications of the birth dying on September 18th. Nineteenth century customs as they were, there was little room for a single father raising a child. Annie was taken to live with her aunt, Caroline Ella Campbell, where she flourished under nurturing hands, leaving a family line that still remembers her today. This was probably for the best as back in Detroit Henry struggled with the loss of his wife and fell into a deep depression of which he carried to his grave.[33,34,35]

For their efforts at Hillsdale College, Brush and Smith were paid $250 and received 2 future scholarships. The scholarship was most definitely meant for Annie, in order to insure that she received a proper education. Alas, it was never used by her or her future half-brother Frederick. It may be still there awaiting a Brush descendent to claim it and fulfill Henry's promise.[36]

As his private life crumbled about him, Henry's career and talent as an architect grew. Perhaps it was this that he held tight to in order to retain his purpose in this world. The small town of Williamston, Michigan, just outside of Michigan's capital Lansing, had inspired the community to fund a grand schoolhouse. They called on the firm of Brush and Smith to design the structure. Using their plans the Williamson School House was constructed in 1875. It was a beautiful Victorian brick building with a stately curved pyramidal dome, containing "four school rooms, two recitation rooms and a public hall on the third floor." Unfortunately, the life of this structure was not long, as it was destroyed by fire in 1887.[37]

Eighteen seventy-five also saw Brush and Smith awarded what would be their largest project ever, the design of the new Detroit Public Library on Gratiot between Farrar and Farmer streets. The construction cost of this structure, completed in 1877, was $150,000. Originally the library was designed with a highly ornamental tower, similar to that of the Williamston School house, "stone steps, and floors in the upper galleries" but these were eliminated due to a lack of public funding.[38,39,40]

Throughout 1875, Henry's career continued to accelerate. Hugh and Henry's office had obtained quite a reputation in Detroit at the time. Young men applying themselves to the profession would forgo opportunities at older, more experienced firms, to work with these fast-rising stars. One such apprentice architect was George Mason. In the second half of 1875 Hugh and Henry split and formed separate firms. Mason originally started his architectural career with Smith's new firm in an effort to learn to design cornices from him, but that only lasted a summer. By fall, Mason had moved to Henry's firm as he thought opportunities were better there. Henry's firm must have initially struggled, either from the split with Smith, or the ongoing economic depression, seeing that Mason worked for nine months there without pay. Mason started out assigned to some specific detailing work on the George O. Robinson House and the Detroit Public Library, two projects left over from the Brush & Smith partnership.[41]

George Mason left the employ of Henry in 1878, and went on to become a prominent architect in Detroit. The firm he subsequently founded lasted, until the 1960's[b]. Early on, Mason gave another young "upstart" a chance at his firm. This budding architect was none other than Albert Kahn, the most famous architect in Detroit and father of the modern automobile plant. The firm Kahn eventually started is still in existence today.[42]

As Henry's firm embarked on the design of the Ransom Gillis House in 1876, Mason had earned the right of equal billing. Most certainly, both had read John Ruskin's earlier work, *The Stones of Venice,* in which he revisited the beautiful architecture of northern Italy. This book was the primary influence responsible for the detailed flow of ele-

---

[b] *The only picture of the Ransom Gillis House as it originally stood is a 3" by 3" snapshot in the Burton Historical Collection at the main branch of the Detroit Public Library. From the writing on the back of this picture and its condition it looks like it was once in a scrapbook belonging to George Mason's firm, probably donated to the Collection as they were liquidating the company.*

ments present in the Ransom Gillis House. From Ruskin's 1853 work:

> *The especial condition of true ornament is, that it be beautiful in its place, and nowhere else, and that it aid the effect of every portion of the building over which is has influence; that it not, by its richness, make other parts bald, or by its delicacy, make other parts coarse. Every one of its qualities has reference to its place and use: and it is fitted for its service by what would be faults and deficiencies if it had no special duty.* [43,44,45]

Ruskin's influence here can easily be seen in the use of the turret with its beautiful stone, tile, and brick details.

In the creative hands of Brush and Mason, the design of the Ransom Gillis House was taken beyond that of the typical Victorian structures of the time. Turrets, like the one of this house, were present in elegant houses of the time both in the Midwest and the East Coast. Of course, Brush and Mason enhanced what was then typical. Where traditional turrets concentrated the onlooker's eyes upward towards the Tower Finial, the Ransom Gillis House's turret added interesting details below. The beautifully ornate base with its quadruplets of flower blossoms, similar but all slightly different, drew ones eyes downward. This pattern continued, though more subtly, to the decorated post that was needed to support the brick of the turret. Add to this, the delicate tile inlay around the equator of this element and the small ornamental columns on the windowsills and the centerpiece of this structure was completely balanced. With this as its anchor, the rest of the structure was designed to flow with it, yet not be overpowered by it. The brickwork details, especially of the chimneys, were typical of elite houses of the day, but elements were subtly added to match the elegance of the turret. Dark ornately carved wood columns protected the entrance and pulled a guest's eyes from the turret as they entered the house. Small bits of delicate tile inlay were scattered throughout the structure, large enough to be seen yet not overwhelming to the centerpiece. Lastly, a steep, dark slate mansard roof with ornate iron cresting completed the peaks in a traditional detail of the day.[46,47]

There are some who believe that the brick masons and other skilled workers used in this construction were ex-slaves, fresh from the South, freed and looking for work after they rode the trains north to Detroit. This could have quite probably been true as prior to the Civil War an estimated 80% of the "artisans" in the South were slaves who obtained their training on plantations.[48] The tile work on the house was accredited by some to Detroit's Pewabic Pottery, but this could not have been so, as the pottery was not founded until some 27 years later.[49] Ironically the Ransom Gillis House, with the unlikely pleasure of having survived over 130 years, actually had the lowest known construction cost, $12,000, of any of Henry's structures.[50]

That same year Henry married Charlotte M. Grosvernor. The next year their first and only child was born, Frederick F. Brush. In 1878 Henry formed a partnership with John M. Donaldson. Whereas Henry was self-taught, Donaldson was fresh back from studies in Munich and Paris, where he had developed what would become a lifelong friendship with American painter Gari Melchers.[51,52,53,54]

------------------------------------------------------------------

A cloudless sky met Henry as he awoke on a warm Monday morning in July of 1879. It was comfortable in the upstairs bedroom, though the temperature was already in the upper 70's. The window curtains fluttered softly as a slight summer breeze entered from the Southwest. Although he had not slept well in weeks, mornings were still his favorite time of day. In the mornings his mind was as

19

clear and peaceful as the cloudless sky, anything seemed possible. This euphoria usually was not sustainable, especially as of late. But this morning was different, he felt especially good, more hours than usual of peaceful sleep last night left him more refreshed, perhaps he would attend the gymnasium twice today. Maybe the recent afternoon trips to the Y.M.C.A. gymnasium, behind the Opera House at Gratiot and Farmer, were the reason he was sleeping better. He enjoyed talking to the other men there and felt like he had accomplished something. Recently he had met another participant at the gymnasium who, after attending there regularly for over two years, had recovered quite well from weakness and chronic disease. He resolved to talk to him that day, as to better inform himself on how he could replicate this task.[55,56,57]

After he ate breakfast, he committed himself to attend the gymnasium this morning as well as this afternoon. Donning his jacket he walked out onto Wayne Street and headed north to Michigan a block and a half away. The Y.M.C.A. was only 7 or 8 blocks away from his house, normally an easy walk, but in his current condition he felt it better to catch the horse car that ran down Michigan Avenue. He boarded the car at Wayne and Michigan, and sat down for the short 3 to 4 block trip. To his right passed L.W. Day's Lumber Yard. He marveled at all the activity of the laborers there. It made him wonder who was really responsible for the rapid growth occurring in the city. He only put pen to paper, these men actually built the structures he envisioned. Further down Michigan the carriage passed Griswold, to the left was his office in Halls Block which he shared with his recently acquired partner John M. Donaldson, maybe soon he would have the energy to return to his drawings and designs. A block further and the horse car had reached Campus Martius, there it turned slightly to the left and headed up Monroe Avenue. It passed the Detroit Opera House on the right. The car proceeded up Monroe one block, and he stepped off at Farmer Street. The Gymnasium was only a half a block away. He worked out as usual with the "wooden dumbbells" for about 45 minutes than retraced his path back home.[58,59,60,61]

Feeling well he returned to the gym that afternoon, around 5 o'clock. Henry joined a small class in the "wooden dumb-bell exercise." He commented to another attendee on his motivations in coming to the gym regularly, "It is not endurance I want so much as resolution to come here every day to practice." Those there with him that afternoon saw this as a positive sign he wanted to better himself, unsuspecting of what lie ahead tomorrow.[62]

Tuesday morning broke hot and muggy as Monday, yet a slightly stronger breeze from the West gave some relief. This would prove not enough for Henry. His current condition and added financial stresses seemed to overwhelm him. He would not go to the gym today. After dinner, he climbed the stairs to his workroom; he told Charlotte he was going to attempt to work on some drawings. After a few minutes, Charlotte went up to check on him. She had been greatly concerned about him lately as he frequently spoke of suicide. Seeing that he seemed fine, consulting a book in his room, she left to attend to her work and Frederick downstairs. That was the last she spoke to him.[63,64,65]

Upon her leaving, Henry removed two revolvers from the desk drawer and slowly positioned himself on the floor of his workroom. The metallic taste of the muzzles he placed in his mouth did not diminish the surges of overwhelming fear that rose up from his chest to his forehead. They kept coming like waves to the ocean shore, pausing momentarily in the trough just long enough to give him a glimmer of hope that the preceding crest would be the last. This would not be so. The heat and humidity of this typical 90° Detroit July afternoon, intensified in this upstairs room,

21

just added to his distress. As the crest of the next wave reached the beads of sweat that had formed on his forehead, he looked over at the table upon which his unfinished drawings lay. Architecture was his passion but he hadn't been able to work for weeks. He convinced himself he would never again have the ability to do so. This only elongated the period of this last crest. He felt nothing of Frederick, Annie, Jeanie, James, Charlotte, William, or even Amanda, only the unending waves. This last one seemed to be taking forever to subside, would it ever? The devil truly does reside in the hippocampus. Suddenly, a great peace came upon him, the waves were gone, not to return, he had made his decision. He was floating, then a slight squeeze, he heard not the blast.[66,67,68]

Charlotte and Mary the servant initially thought nothing of the sound, they assumed it had come from outdoors, but when Charlotte took Frederick upstairs, they found him. Charlotte felt disturbingly calm at the sight of what was once her husband lying there; a pool of blood engulfing what remained of the back of his skull. She strangely expected as much, considering his actions over the past six weeks. Maybe now the demons were finally not terrorizing him anymore. All she could do was stare at the body. Luckily Frederick was only two, he would not remember. Mary ran from the room, horrified at the scene and quickly called for Dr. Brodie a few houses down. Upon arrival, Dr. Brodie felt the need to probe, like some type of analytical investigation was required to determine the cause of death, the holes in the roof of the victim's mouth far into the anterior portions of his brain. He was attempting to find the metal balls that had caused this damage. None were found.[69,70]

Thus ended the life of one Henry T. Brush, a talented, promising and prolific young Detroit architect, 29 years of age, on July 15, 1879 at about 2 O'clock in the afternoon.

   The weather on Thursday the 17th was quite different than the days proceeding, cool and clear, a front was coming down from Canada, it was like a page of a book had turned. When they emerged from the First Congregational Church following Henry's casket, the temperature was 70. Quite odd for mid-July, but then this was a different type of day. As they loaded him in to the carriage, drawn by two elegant black horses, Charlotte with Frederick in her arms, climbed into the carriage behind that carrying Henry. William and Henry's business partner John Donaldson also climbed in, they did not want her to ride alone. There were only two Protestant cemeteries in Detroit, the old Elmwood Cemetery out Lafayette, and the new Woodmere Cemetery less than three-quarters of a mile down Fort Street in Springwell Township. Henry was buried at Woodmere; after all that was where Jeanie lay.[71,72,73]

   Upon arrival they laid him down to the left of Jeanie, it seemed suitable. The identical headstones read:[74]

| HENRY T. BRUSH | JEANIE F. CAMPBELL |
|:---:|:---:|
| AUG. 9, 1849 | WIFE OF |
| JULY 15,1879 | HENRY T. BRUSH |
| | DEC. 28, 1853 |
| | SEPT. 18, 1874 |

   Just three years later, all returned to Woodmere to bid goodbye to Henry's stepfather and mentor William Cicero Grant, who had spent his last years at Harper Hospital. They laid him down next to Amanda, both just a few steps in front of Henry and Jeanie. It seemed as if the magic of their accomplishments were buried with them.[75,76]

------------------------------------------------------------------------

Three years later, on November 30th, 1882, Charlotte married Henry's last business partner, John M. Donaldson. By the time Henry's son Frederick was a teenager he had two stepbrothers, Alexander 7 years his younger and Bruce 14 years his younger. They all lived at 139 Alfred Street just a block from the Ransom Gillis House. Due to this age difference it was unlikely that Frederick spent much time playing with his stepbrothers. Instead, Frederick could have very well made friends with Gaylord Gillis, son of Ransom, who was just 3 years his senior.[77,78,79,80]

John and Charlotte insured that Frederick obtained a proper education, but one can only wonder about how much he knew of his father. Frederick attended public school, and by 1896 he was a consulting engineer in Detroit. He worked for the Sprague Electric Elevator Company in Detroit and spent a two-year stint with the Sprague Company in Paris. He returned to Detroit in 1902, and established himself as a consulting engineer in the firm of Brush, Allen & Anderson. Interestingly Frederick's hobby at the time was photography taking after his Uncle James. A year after returning from France, Frederick married Bessie Giddings, who had resided with her parents just a few years earlier at 121 Alfred Street.[81,82,83]

Frederick and Bessie lived in a number of residences in Detroit and the suburbs over the next few years. As Detroit "filled up" during this period of increasing industrialization, this young couple had an option not available to most of the working class in the city, they could easily move to the "open" lands out West. Surprisingly Frederick and Bessie exercised this option in a very dramatic way. Sometime after 1908 they moved to Earlimart, California on the semi-arid plains 40 miles north of Bakersfield. There they became farmers. This flat, treeless plain, with its stifling, dry heat at the foot of the Sierras was a far cry from the summer humidity and winter snows of Detroit. This move proved a disaster for the young couple, and they were gone from Earlimart by 1915. This failure was most likely due to the rapidly falling water table in the area that also spelled the demise of the nearby town of Allensworth, the first in California to be founded and governed by Black Americans, under the leadership of ex-slave and Union Army officer Colonel Allen Allensworth.[84,85,86]

Bessie disappeared during their time at Earlimart. Frederick surfaced in 1920 as a widower in Los Angeles. We can only guess on how Bessie died, no doubt from illness, accident, or in childbirth, on the farm in Earlimart. Falling back on his training as an engineer, Frederick found himself living alone in a boarding house in L.A. Frederick never returned to Detroit and died in Los Angeles in 1942 at the age of 65. Ironically, this ease of mobility facilitated the loss of his roots and his disappearance from human memory like what had happened earlier to his father.[87]

Brother James also moved west. He left his studio in Detroit around 1874 for better opportunities in Minneapolis. There he established a successful photography business, and trained his two sons Edward and Bert in the process. He died in 1906 at the age of 60. Edward practiced the art in Minneapolis for the rest of his life. His younger brother Bert took advantage of the unfilled opportunities in the West and started a photography studio in Everett, Washington in 1903. Surprisingly just a few minutes from this author's home.[88]

Deep in the catacombs beneath a 1905 building on Hewitt Avenue in Everett, Washington I found myself in a small room that looked out upon a cement wall. This was home to the files of The Museum of Snohomish County History. Along the wall were plain, yet neatly ordered, beige file cabinets, some of which had not been opened in years. In these common containers laid much of what was left of the work of Henry's nephew, Bert Brush. The curator of this quaint museum, held a small piece of paper in his hand. I watched as he rustled through this meticulously codified repository and pulled out a seemingly endless series of documents and photos. He was giddy with the fact that someone was actually interested in seeing them. Out came a self-portrait of Bert Brush, a handsome man with a friendly full square face, seemingly equally comfortable in a courtroom or local saloon. He was pictured in a turn of the century period gentlemen's suit with a striped tie, and a cigar in his right hand. His fingernails were stained due to years of raw exposure to the silver nitrate of photography. With this face, stories were surely in the offing. His grandson told of Bert's solution to an unsettled stomach in those days. It seems he would treat himself by using what was readily available, Hypo "fixer" solution from his darkroom. Hypo, or sodium thiosulfate, though not possessing serious toxicity would "cause purging" if ingested. We will let the reader imagine what happened after Bert took one of the doses of this "medicine." Most of Bert's 2200 glass negatives, depicting Pacific Northwest life at the beginning of the 20th century, were stored beneath an Everett building for some 60 years. Unfortunately the majority of these were destroyed by the elements and grandchildren who, "washed off the film, and made little windows out of them."[89,90,91,92]

Bert Brush died having no sons and with Frederick Brush being a widower in Los Angeles, the Brush family name vanished as it was carried to the West coast.

-----------------------------------------------------------------

Upon my initial investigations into the history of Henry T. Brush, the easiest to be found were descendents of Charlotte his second wife. The chronicler of this side of the family's history knew very little of Henry, stating simply that he was "quite an elusive character." This was to be expected, as most of Charlotte's life was spent married to John Donaldson, not Henry. On Henry's first wife's side, the

Campbell's, information was somewhat more complete, perhaps since some of the descendents of his daughter Annie Frances still lived in the Detroit area, yet they knew little of his architecture. It had been less than 125 years. The ink was still fresh on the records of this time. Why was there such a "Forgetting?"

Again we return to the ease and efficiency of mobility in the United States over the last 150 years. Why did Frederick and Bessie suddenly up and move from Detroit where they had lived all their lives to start again as farmers on the unfamiliar arid plains of south-central California? Were their monetary concerns? Were there other situations that drove them from Detroit? Whichever the case, it was relatively simple for them to "re-make" themselves in what would be considered in most other parts of the world as a "far away land." In almost all other areas of the world, this type of movement would have been drastically more difficult due to national borders, language barriers, social barriers, and the like. But having remade North America with a uniform European model, this type of movement was easily facilitated. Most government policy in this country over the last 200 years had promoted this fluidity. It is true that throughout time people had ventured to new areas, but it should be remembered that this expansion was usually done by only a few adventurous individuals, with a significant portion of the population following them very slowly and only after a very long period of time. Movements in the U.S. have been at light-speed in comparison.

In most areas outside the Americas, and North America especially, the easily habitable areas were "filled up" long ago. In most other locations in the world, people have been forced to either learn to live with one another or continue in a destructive cycle of violence. Much of Europe and Asia chose to limit their individual freedom to accommodate their finite resources. To Americans, limiting individual freedom was quite a stifling prospect, almost impossible to except. The seemingly endless amount of unoccupied land and cheap resources available in North America in the 19th Century led us to a mindset that this would always be the case. There was no reason for us to limit ourselves. Immigrants had flocked here throughout the years with this specific ideal in mind. American's seemed then, as now, to find a significant amount of identity and security in believing they had this migration opportunity available to them, whether they chose to exercise it or not. In most other areas of the world this freedom of movement was not an option, but then again neither would have been the abandonment of structures like the Ransom Gillis House and areas like Brush Park.

------------------------------------------------------------------

On July 12th, 2005, the world watched as the 76th All-Star Game was played at Comerica Park in downtown Detroit. Just 350 yards northwest up John R stood the turret leaning so precariously off the corner of the Ransom Gillis House, all memories of the life of its creator, Henry T. Brush, faded away in Americans' overarching desire and ability to transplant, transform, and recreate themselves.

# Blue Bloods & Blood Lines

*"As no gentleman will drop into a chair before a lady is seated, so in calling, after rising when the lady enters, let her indicate your seat, wait until she is seated, and then seat yourself. Most ladies have their favorite seat, and perhaps a fancy (who knows?) for the light that strikes them just there."*

--- Detroit blue book : a society directory for the city of Detroit,
Detroit Free Press Pub. Co., 1885[1]

As they laid Henry down next to his first love, the land upon which the Ransom Gillis House still stands was part of the Estate of Edmond A. Brush (no relation to Henry T.) The house's namesake, Ransom Gillis, a wholesale dry goods merchant,[2] and his wife Helen started living there sometime after April 20, 1878, when a building permit was taken out for its construction. Interestingly, the Gillis', though their name in recent times has been tied to the structure, lived there for only a little over two years. On 9/3/1880, Helen Gillis sold the house and property to Mary M. Stinchfield. Helen did not actually obtain the deed for this property from the Estate of Edmond A. Brush until four days prior to its sale to the Stinchfields. The Gillis' probably had not yet fully paid off the note on the property and had to do so prior to the sale. The architectural firm of Mason & Rice (remember George Mason worked for Henry T. Brush on the design of the Ransom Gillis House) took out a building permit on June 6, 1881 for the plot of land right next door at 69 Alfred Street. There the Gillis' built a house in which they lived for the next 34 years. It is not surprising that we would end up calling the structure at the corner of Alfred and John R under what now seems to be an erroneous name, as prominent houses of the late 1800's were named for the person who originally contracted their building.[3,4,5,6]

Though it seems odd that the Gillis' would move so close, it must be understood that the Brush Park area was a congregating point for the "Blue Bloods" of the time, especially along Alfred Street. This location was close enough to the bustling city center where the residents of Alfred Street would go to attend to their businesses, yet it was still far enough away from the working water front of the Detroit River where the growing numbers of unskilled and semi-skilled laborers worked and lived. Still in 1880 Detroit's population was only 116,340, rating it 18th in the country, holding only a tenth of the population of New York, one-eight of Philadelphia's, a fifth of Chicago's, and less than that of Cleveland or Jersey City, NJ. More importantly, the growth rate of population in Detroit was stable and would remain so till the end of the 19th Century. The same was not true for other large cities of the time. In Chicago the population growth rate spiked significantly for the first time in the 1880's, while in New York it spiked in the 1890's. Over the course of the European immigration into the United States, four cities, New York, Chicago, Detroit, and Los Angeles, experienced changes in population growth rates significantly greater than anywhere else. New York experienced changes in growth rates that far exceeded any American city, while Chicago, Detroit, and Los Angeles saw very similar maximum growth rates, though they occurred at different times. Chicago's occurred initially in the 1880's, Detroit's occurred in the 1910's and Los Angeles' occurred in the 1920's. The timing of these initial growth spurts, and the demographic and economic conditions under which they occurred helped dictate the futures of these four metropolises. Detroiters had no reason to worry about their city's future at the end of the 19th Century though, living, especially for the affluent, was easy. Manageable population growth allowed the Gillis' and their "Blue Blood" neighbors on Alfred Street to live comfortably in their convenient enclave within a short carriage ride of the Detroit Opera House and the other amenities of the city. This situation remained intact into the second decade of the 20th Century, allowing this to be, at least for a time, the Golden Age of Alfred Street.[7]

"Blue Bloods" lived on this section of Alfred Street, between Woodward Avenue and Brush Street, from the 1870's to the late 1910's. More specifically, the Ransom Gillis House at 63 Alfred Street was occupied by this affluent class from 1876 till 1919. During these 43 years four families owned the house:

| | | |
|---|---|---|
| The Gillis' | 1876 – 9/3/1880 | 4 Years |
| The Stinchfield's | 9/3/1880 – 4/26/1888 | 8 Years |
| The Fox's | 4/26/1888 – 6/6/1916 | 28 Years |
| The Fikes' | 6/6/1916 – 7/22/1919 | 3 Years |

The Fikes actually lived in the house, presumably under a land contract, for a number of years prior to purchasing it. Thus some of the 28 years in which the house was owned by the Fox's it was actually occupied by the Fikes. In addition, the Drake family occupied the house for a short time between the Fox's and the Fikes, but never owned it.

When Mary M. Stinchfield purchased the house at 63 Alfred Street in 1880 this area of Detroit was embarking on 30 years of prosperity of which it would never see again. Mary's husband Charles was a lumberman with an office close by at 5 Merrill Block.[8] This was a common business of the day as the primeval forests in Lower Michigan were not yet completely gone. Life in this enclave of high 19th Century society would have seemed foreign and pretentious to us today as well as it must have to the working class people who labored just a short distance away at the City's water-front.

In those days "Society Directories" were printed. Unlike City Directories that listed the names of all residents and businesses in the city, these Society Directories only listed the names of "Prominent Citizens" and were to "be of service to them in their business as well as their social affairs."[9] Some of the etiquette information contained in these books can give us an idea of the customs and interactions that occurred within this privileged class. The etiquette surrounding the use of "Calling Cards" was particularly interesting. Calling cards, kind of like business cards but used in social situations, were usually handed to the domestic servant that answered the door. The Ransom Gillis House always had at least two live-in domestic servants throughout this time. The 1885 edition of the *Detroit Blue Book: A Society Directory*, in which both Charles Stinchfield and his wife are listed at 63 Alfred Street, had 8 pages devoted solely to calling card etiquette:

> *Cards may talk, or say nothing---of any consequence. Hence the card language, which lends significance and saves time, trouble and instructions to servants.*
>
> *Cards should never be other than in plain "script" letter, without flourishes. The upper right corner turned down means "visit." The lower right corner, "adieu." The upper left corner, "congratulations." The lower left corner, "condolence." The entire left end, "the ladies of the family"---not including lady guests.[10]*

And while the husbands were away at the office:

> *Gentlemen will never leave a card on a lady only---if she have a husband. He must also have a card. Otherwise*

32

*it implies a certain special attention to the lady, and a slight to the husband.*[11]

If you wanted to play matchmaker for a female single friend of yours:

> *A lady wishing to notify her friends of a lady visitor in the family should send her own card and that of her visitor in the same envelope. If instead of this an entertainment is given to meet the guest a call on the stranger afterward should be made.*
>
> *Gentlemen visiting a lady acquaintance in a family with which the caller is unacquainted, should send a card to the lady of the house as well as to the guest.*[12]

When your daughter's date came over there were slightly more formalities to consider then simply honking the horn in the driveway:

> *A call made by a young man upon the daughter of a family should include the mother, or chaperone pro tem. The hostess may or may not make her appearance; the name of the visitor will probably decide this. Abroad, if not present she would probably be in a communicating room. A single card sent in with the entire left end turned down (which exceptionally to the rule one might do in such a case), of an inquiry for "the ladies" would include also the objective point --- the daughter. The astonishment of foreigners who come to this country is unbounded, that they can call upon a young lady and pass an hour or two with her alone --- perhaps even without knowing the mother.*[13]

In 1888 the Stinchfields sold the Ransom Gillis House to Alanson J. Fox. Alanson typified the Blue Bloods of the time, educated, wealthy, and influential, with family roots deep in the "New World."[14]

It was a clear pleasantly warm spring day in Detroit when Alanson J. Fox age 55 purchased the Ransom Gillis House entering into an extended period of time, some 15 years, in which the life inside this structure truly reflected its architecture. Alanson and his family, wife Cornelia, sons Stuart and Alan, and daughter Julia were not of Michigan lineage. They had come to Detroit only to be closer to Alanson's latest lumber business investment in the town of Manistique in the Upper Peninsula of Michigan. Alanson had spent the majority of his adult life in Painted Post, NY. Matter of fact, the Fox family actually kept their roots in New York state, many of them who left returning and those who did not still considering it their home even to this day.[15,16] Alanson's roots ran deep in this country, deep for a European that is. His ancestors arrived in the New World sometime prior to 1675. The wealth that allowed Alanson to acquire the grand house on the corner of John R and Alfred Street was in no small way a result of his family's legacy of "making use" of this North American continent. His great-grandfather Daniel Fox, a farmer, tanner, and shoe maker, was the first to attain a recordable amount of wealth in the New World when he purchased 170 acres of land near Canaan, New York in 1779. Much land was available as, "the country about Canaan was new and sparsely settled at the time." Of course the land on the Eastern Seaboard was far from "new" as Native Americans had populated it for thousands of years. Alanson's great-grandfather was an officer in the Revolutionary as well as the French and Indian War. His grandfather as well as four of his great uncles also fought in the Revolutionary War.[17]

The lumber business, which had brought Alanson J. Fox his wealth and facilitated his movement to Detroit, was a direct legacy of this father Norman Fox. Norman and his brother Alanson (Alanson J.'s Uncle) originally started several businesses together in Warren County, New York, not far from where their ancestor Daniel had originally homesteaded in the late 1700's. The Fox Family had long been a presence in this area of the Adirondack's in upstate New York. Norman's father, Baptist Reverend Jehiel Fox, was credited with being the founder of Chestertown in this area. It was there that these two brothers entered into their first business venture together, a tavern. One would wonder whether this was a tavern in the sense we would think of presently, as the serving of alcohol in this establishment would not be consistent with the Fox Family Baptist roots. As of this time, around 1809, the Fox brothers had not as of yet entered into the lumber business. This is not to say that they did not participate in European "use" of the land in ways never contemplated by the indigenous population. Along with the tavern they also ran an ashery on their property. Asheries have all but disappeared from our modern memory, but they facilitated the destruction of much of the primordial hardwoods, especially elms, in the Northeast long before logging softwoods for lumber took place. In the late 1700's and the early 1800's Potash, potassium carbonate, was exported in great quantities from the colonies to England and the rest of Europe, where it was required in the glass and ceramic industries. Adding potassium carbonate to silica sand reduced the melting point of the resulting glass mix making it much easier to process. By burning hardwoods and boiling the resulting ash, crude Potash could be extracted from the resulting liquid. The Potash industry was so important in New York that it funded the purchase of much of the farmland in this area. So important was this industry that the first U.S. patent was issued on this subject. This use of the land was short-lived though as potassium compounds soon became readily available from mined mineral deposits and evaporation of saline bodies of water. Unfortunately, this was only after the obliteration of much of the old growth hardwoods in Upstate New York.[18,19,20,21,22]

It was then that Alanson and Norman Fox turned their efforts towards the lumber industry. Though hardwoods were scarce, there were lots of pines to be cut. Softwoods had been spared in the Potash business because they produced such a small amount of ash. The Fox brothers in about 1820 started taking pines from the Adirondacks near the towns of Athol and Johnsburgh and floated them down the Hudson River to Glen Falls. Thus started the Fox involvement in lumbering which eventually reached from there to southern New York, Michigan, and eventually to California and Oregon. Along with their business success the Fox Brothers had active public lives in their community serving as Justices of the Peace, local Supervisors, and even in the New York State Legislature. [23,24,25]

As the pines thinned in the Adirondacks Norman, without his brother Alanson who died in 1829, needed to find a new location. He and two partners settled on Painted Post in the south central region of New York state some 200 miles to the west-southwest. Here they formed the lumber firm of Fox, Weston, & Bronson which Alanson J. eventually became a part of.[26,27]

Alanson J. Fox the longest and perhaps the most prominent owner of the Ransom Gillis House, spent only the last years of his long and eventful life there. In his early 20's Alanson started work for his father's company, Fox, Weston & Bronson in Painted Post. He remained part of this company for the next 55 years. To get a true feeling for a person and the times they lived, there is nothing more valuable than their own words. Here we are lucky as Alanson J. Fox was an educated man who left behind a number of letters and speeches that provide a clear window into his mind.[28]

We first find Alanson J. Fox at age 27 held up in the Irons Hotel in Kingston, Ontario, Canada. There he worked at Brewer's Mills a lumber mill on the Rideau Canal owned by Fox & Anglin.[29] Whether Alanson ever actually labored in the sawmills is not known, but by this time he was firmly involved in the management end of the business. In a manner similar to people of today, Alanson showed his youthful drive to succeed and impatience with those who did not share his Protestant work ethic. In a letter written to his brother dated December 15, 1860 he was quite irritated at the slow pace of negotiations he was conducting on his father's behalf:

> Dr Brother.
>
> I am waiting patiently here for the world to move a little faster, am getting tired and uneasy at the dull slow movement of the clock & the duller, slower movements of every man who does business in this city of stone. At home when I have a great deal to do I can get up early & work hard & crowd off business but here I have to wait the motion of the elements, get up at 8 o'clock to breakfast, wait until 10 o'clock before I can see anybody, then talk a few minutes & wait another 24 hours.
>
> I am ready to make a solemn vow that if I ever can unravel this twisted mess of business to which Father is so unfortunately fastened I will never show my face this side of the line again.[a]
>
> ....
>
> I have a great deal of trouble in closing up Father's old business here. Mr. A tries as hard as he can to make matters worse, obstinately refuses to pay any part of his honest debt to Father & throws every possible stumbling block in the way of any feasible plan for the payment of the debts. There are about $6000 (converts to $150,000 to $ 300,000 in today's dollars depending how you calculate it)[30] of debts to pay which we could nearly wipe out with the mill property if Mr. A would only cooperate with us in the matter. Instead of that he is aiming to make us pay off the debt & leave the whole mill property to him.

---

[a] *Canadian border.*

*But then I am not discouraged. Even if everything here proves a total loss we have enough left at home to pay off everything & have considerable left but it is hard to work like a nigger for several years to pay up old scores. I can make money enough at the Post to pay off father's debts if they were twice as large.*

*I have done a good deal of hard work & had a good deal of bitter experience in this Canada scrape for one of my age but I find it has sharpened my wits & opened my eyes enough to help me a good deal in doing business at P Post without making mistakes.*[31]

Two years later when the Civil War broke out the Fox family responded as they had in all prior conflicts on North American soil. All four of Alanson's brothers, William, Charlie, Norman, and George fought for the Union. Alanson did not enlist, as he was needed to mind the family business. This is not to say that he was not involved in the war effort as "no man in the county did more than he in support of the government in the raising of troops and in the looking after of the interests of the soldiers in the field."[32] The Civil War was much more personal than American conflicts of today. Friends and family visited soldiers in the field. Mothers came to camp and cared for their injured or sick sons; maybe this brought the misery close enough to home to help mitigate the length of the conflict. Alanson wrote a letter to his uncle detailing a visit he made to an encampment outside of Harpers Ferry where his brothers William and Charlie were located. His letter dated October 15, 1862 placed the Union camp at Maryland Heights where they had retreated to after being driven from Harpers Ferry by Confederate troops under the command of Stonewall Jackson.[33] This was almost 3 years to the day after the violent abolitionist John Brown and his small band of men raided the armory at Harper's Ferry in an effort to trigger a slave revolt in the South. Though unsuccessful in his plan Brown's actions fertilized the seeds that led to the conflict that had brought Alanson and his brothers to this hill overlooking the town.[34] (John Brown's connections to Detroit were in the past, associated with freeing slaves via the Underground Railroad. Alanson's involvement with Detroit, unbeknownst to him at the time lay in the future and his life-long quest for timber.)

...

*I found William in Washington looking better than I expected and after staying with him there a few days I went to his regiment with him.*

*He is far from being well but thinks he can stand it.*

*Charlie is well and looks black and tough and dirty and happy. I staid* (sp.) *in camp so long that I gave up the idea of coming home via New York and come directly home.*

*The Regt were encamped on the Maryland Heights opposite Harpers Ferry. This morning we learn by letters from some of his company that William is not as well as when I left.*

*Mr. Bronson's Son (of Fox, Weston, & Bronson) who is 2nd Lieut in the company is very sick with typhoid fever and his mother has gone to take care of him.*

*There were a good many officers and men in the Regt sick when I was there and they all look very different from the men who left Elmira* (near Painted Post) *2 months ago with new uniforms and great expectations.*

...

*A.J. Fox*[35]

After the war Alanson remained in Painted Post, and was by then a partner in Fox, Weston, & Bronson. In the following years, he more than any of his brothers, remained closely involved with lumber manufacturing and profited quite well from it. By 1870 Alanson, then 36 years old, had a net worth of $ 12,000 (similar to being worth $ 2.5 MM in

2006)[36] and was living with his first wife Abie, their two children and two Domestic Servants in Painted Post. Living right next door was Abijah Weston with whom Alanson would partner as they expanded their lumber interests west into Michigan.[37]

A little over a year later and 550 miles due west, a fire started in the alley behind 137 DeKoven Street in Chicago. This far away event triggered Alanson's final venture in the lumber business that brought him to the house at 63 Alfred Street in Detroit. On Sunday, October 8, 1871 the Great Chicago Fire started and by the time it burn itself out a day later one-third of the city's 300,000 residents were homeless. Large amounts of lumber were required for the reconstruction that started almost immediately.[38] Much of this lumber to rebuild the city along with that needed to open up the vast, tree-less, Great Plains just to the southwest, would come from Michigan. In the meantime, as the accessible lumber in Painted Post became exhausted, the owners of Fox, Weston & Bronson were forced to look West for fresh resources. What they found was the Chicago Lumbering Company of Manistique[b], Michigan on the northern shore of Lake Michigan. The Chicago Lumbering Company had been in existence in one form or another since 1860 and had passed through the hands of various owners, none of which had the means to exploit this virgin resource to its fullest extent. The opportunity was perfect for people with capital. The generations of lumbering in New York State had provided this capital to those in Painted Post. With Abijah Weston supplying the major financial backing, in 1872 Alanson and a few other "York Staters" (as they would come to be known) purchased the Chicago Lumbering Company. Much of the initial lumber from their mill on the banks of the Manistique River was used to rebuild Chicago. The pines immediately around Manistique were quickly removed;

---

[b] Called Epsport originally

as Abijah was most fearful of fire destroying his newly acquired assets. Soon after clear-cut deforestation expanded to the surrounding area. Initially logs were transported to the mill in Manistique via the vast watershed of the Manistique River, but as the source of trees moved farther and farther away from the water, transporting the raw logs became a problem. To this end the Chicago Lumbering Company formed the Manistique & Northwestern Railway of which Alanson served as president for a time. Alanson and Abijah never lived with their families in Manistique, Abijah remained in New York and Alanson eventually moved to Detroit.[39]

With the "York Staters" came expansion of not only the lumber industry but of the town itself. Along with the surrounding forest land the Chicago Lumbering Company owned almost the whole town of Manistique. Enforcement of the moral values of the owners came along with this monopoly. Resultantly, the town was "dry" for a time. "Any property they leased or later sold had a covenant attached to it saying that the premises could not manufacture, store, or sell intoxicating liquors."[40] One of the biggest proponents of this was none other than the devout Baptist Alanson J. Fox. As with most attempts to legislate morality, Alanson's hold on the town's morals was short-lived. Alanson's nemesis came in the form of one Daniel Heffron, who in the 1880's bought one of the only parcels of land in town not owned by the company. He quickly opened a saloon and gambling room on the property. Alanson could do nothing as only his religious ideals, not any government laws, had been violated. Seeing an opening and an obvious market in the community (not that much different than the market those in Painted Post had seen in the trees around Manistique 10 years prior) numerous others followed Heffron's lead. A number of saloons quickly sprung up on the limited non-company land in the area. Heffron, not satisfied with the saloon and gambling, soon moved into prostitution. But this endeavor ran him up against the law as well as the churches. After a few run-ins with the authorities and a bout of bribery and intimidation of jurors, Heffron's luck ran out in Manistique and he was forced to escape further west to avoid imprisonment. Though Alanson had won this battle, he lost the war and the Chicago Lumbering Company's efforts to keep Manistique "dry" were gone forever.[41]

By the early 1900's, with the economically accessible pines dwindling in Manistique, the owners at the time sold off their assets in the Chicago Lumbering Company to the Consolidated Lumber Company. Though the "York Staters" were gone, they left their mark on the area's land and the water. During their operation, the Chicago Lumbering Company and the other lumber companies in the area (at their peak a total of five were running) found that the easiest way to dispose of their sawdust was to simply dump it into the Manistique River. By the early 1880's the amount of sawdust settling in the river had formed a sandbar aptly named Abijah's Island. Eventually this sawdust reached Lake Michigan and by the 1890's covered the shoreline for 20 miles in either direction, obliterating the local fishery. This legacy of Alanson and his partners' remains to this day in the sawdust tides. Little known to those outside the area and a mystery to the urban escapees that eventually built vacation homes on the lake, is the yearly occurrence of the sawdust tides that cover the beaches near Manistique. Thirty years ago when children went out for a swim in the lake they would have to wade out until they were waist deep before they cleared the floating sawdust. When the winds and currents are right, sawdust deposited in the lake some 100 years ago still makes its annual appearance on the shore. Alanson and his partners at Chicago Lumbering viewed the environment as endless, at least in its ability to absorb any wastes they produced.[42,43,44]

Today we can look with 20/20 hindsight at the actions of Alanson and his fellow "Lumber Barons" in the area around Manistique and laden their memory with the shame brought about by greed, but this would not be entirely fair. Closer to the truth would be that Alanson and those who worked with and for him simply did not know any better. The facts show that fish probably were the greatest victims of these endeavors. Mainly by the smothering of their spawning and feeding grounds with unimaginable amounts of sawdust, but also via dredging of streams and rivers and filling of wetlands to facilitate the infrastructure to support this industry. It is also true that with the wholesale removal of pines in Michigan the loggers removed one of the only species that could flourish in the poor sandy soils deposited by the last Ice Age. This left the farmers that filled in behind them a far poorer chance of making a go of it than their brethren in Ohio, Indiana, or the Great Plains. Glaciers had never scraped away the ground that far south leaving the soil much richer. But the landowner or logger of the time knew none of this, they just knew that the growing country needed lumber and there seemed to be an endless supply of it right in front of them. Thus:

> ... the 'timber barons' -wealthy as many of them became- were driven as often by altruism as by greed. The 'rapacity' they have been accused of was more often ignorance – ignorance, carelessness, and a misplaced confidence in the exhaustlessness of forests whose beginnings had not been seen and whose end could therefore not possibly be imagined.[45]

Interestingly, once the lumber ran out in the Upper Peninsula one of the owners of the Chicago Lumbering Company, William E. Wheeler, turned his sights even further west because of "the fine timber of that section attracted his attention, and soon afterward he began making purchases in California and Oregon."[46]

Though the Chicago Lumbering Company was purchased by the "York Staters" in 1872, and no doubt Alanson spent a significant amount of time in Manistique in support of it, he did not move his family out of Painted Post until 1888. On April 26th of that year Alanson J. Fox purchased the Ransom Gillis House on the corner of John R and Alfred Street in Detroit Michigan some 380 miles from his current business in Manistique and about the same distance from the place he had called home for the majority of his life. By the time Alanson and his family took up residence at 63 Alfred Street his ancestors had already been in North America for over 213 years, had men who fought in every conflict since the French & Indian War, and were even distant relatives of President George Washington. Matter of fact, some in the Fox family contest that they can trace their lineage back all the way to the first Holy Roman Emperor Charlemagne himself.[47,48]

While involved with the lumbering in Manistique Alanson "transacted all his business affairs from his home at 63 Alfred Street."[49] By the time Alanson had moved to Detroit he was well connected in religious, political, and business circles in Michigan as well as New York State. Alanson's attachment to the Baptist faith originated with his grandfather Reverend Jehiel Fox. Along with being instrumental in the control of liquor and saloons in Manistique, Alanson was also a prominent member and trustee of the Woodward Baptist Church in Detroit. Though he never attended formal school after the age of 16 he had an extensive library at his house on Alfred Street and was involved in a number of institutions of higher learning. Specifically he was a trustee of Kalamazoo College, Rochester Theological Seminary (now part of Rochester University), Rochester University, and Vassar College. It has been said that his library at 63 Alfred Street was quite impressive. One can just imagine Alanson sitting at his desk in his beautifully hardwood appointed Library surrounded by his impressive collection of books on any subject. There at this desk he could be found either working on financial papers for his business dealings in Manistique or writing one of his speeches for which he had become well known.[50,51] Luckily, a number of Alanson's speeches have survived, ones actually written by his own hand probably at his desk on Alfred Street.

One of his speeches, *Taxation and Tariffs, Detroit Home and Day School, March 26, 1897,* tackled the subject of Free Trade and Protection of Domestic Industries. The issues that he elaborated on here were the same that we discuss today when speaking of the WTO or NAFTA, but then the cheap labor was coming from England, France, and Canada, not China, Mexico, and India. Alas, the argument was the same. Alanson came down on the side of Free Trade as our present day impressions of a man of wealth may assume, but he did so lightly, understanding the reasons and motivations of those with an opposing point of view. This trait prevailed in all of Alanson's speeches, he went to great lengths to explain and understand the platform of those on the other side. In the end though Alanson based his support for free trade on the simple fact (in his mind) that protecting domestic markets was not "fair" to all American's as it benefited the few at the cost of the many. From his speech:

> *When General Hancock was running for President he remarked to a reporter in an unguarded moment that the 'tariff was a local issue' and was overwhelmed with ridicule. The General may have ... 'better than he knew' but now no one would question the truth in the statement. Pennsylvania wants high tariff on coal ..., New England want(s) free coal, Troy* (New York) *wants high tariff on collars cuffs, ... Mich*(igan) *lumbermen want high tariff on lumber but low tariff on saws and belts....*
>
> ....
>
> *... a host of Mich*(igan) *Republicans who in past years have shouted themselves hoarse over the necessity of protecting the laborers in Mich*(igan) *woods against the 'cheap labor' of Canada have changed their tune since their Mich*(igan) *pine has been cut off and they have invested their capital in Ca-*

*nadian lumbermen and at the last session of Congress used*
*every possible exertion against a duty on Canadian lumber.*[52]

Earlier in the speech there was a short passage that provided a superb illustration of the impression that America was endless and one could just "move on" once an area had been "used up." It read:

> *They believe (Free Trade advocates) that our fertile soil, our*
> *magnificent water powers, our vast expanse of accessible*
> *cheap lands, our cheap food, our cheap homes, our inventive*
> *genius and the energy and enthusiasm of the Ameri-*
> *can character will more than offset the difference in the cost*
> *of labor.*[53]

Six months earlier Alanson penned Two speeches, *Political Sound Money Talks, October 6, 1896, Majestic Building, Detroit,* and a speech with no title, just prior to the Presidential election that dealt with the question of allowing coinage in silver as well as gold. This was a central element of the 1896 presidential campaign between William McKinley (Republican) and William Jennings Bryan (Democrat). Though Alanson was a staunch Democrat, he split from the party platform, as many Democrats did at the time, over the subject of "Free Silver." The debate over "Free Silver" or the free coinage of money in silver along with gold was the subject of both of these speeches. Basically the "Free Silver" platform was to allow making money out of silver as well as gold and tying the value of this silver coinage to a set amount of gold (16 oz. of silver equal to 1 oz. of gold). This ratio would have to remain constant for the system to work. Unfortunately the price of metal fluctuates via the law of Supply and Demand. At the time large discoveries of silver were made in the West. This would of course have depressed the price of silver. If it were tied permanently to gold at 16 to 1, then silver coins would have been worth more than they were supposed to. Thus a borrower could repay a $100 loan taken out in gold coin originally with $100 of silver coin that only had the purchasing power of say $50. If this held true, the establishment of "Free Silver" as the Democrats favored, would have benefited the borrower at the expense of the lender. It also favored miners in the West, as they would get paid more than the "market price" for the silver they dug up. "Free Silver" horrified industrialists in the Northeast, as they feared it would reduce their investment income. Debtors, mainly in the Midwest, South, and West obviously favored "Free Silver" as it would have instantly reduced what they owed.[54]

Alanson, in these speeches saw Bryan's "election and the success of the principles and the associates with which he is linked would bring untold disaster upon this country."[55] In customary Alanson fashion he was apologetic of his position and respectful of those who held an opposing point of view. From the untitled speech:

> *I come relying on your courtesy to give me a respectful hearing whether you agree with me or not. I may say many things distasteful to some of you. But in whatever I may say I want it distinctly understood in the entirety I will not cast any ridicule or ... on any man's matters. I accord to every man the right which I claim for myself to do his own thinking and to talk and to vote as he thinks for the best interests of the people.*[56]

In the final analysis, Alanson came to his conclusion in support of the "Gold Standard" and rejection of "Free Silver" on the basis of simple fairness. Though Alanson's arguments were steeped in the religious and patriotic rhetoric of the day, proclaiming that adherence to the "Gold Standard" was for "National Honor," he was basically opposed to arbitrarily devaluating a man's possessions whether rich or poor.

In the greater sense the campaign for "Free Silver" was a way to battle the depression of the 1890's. Though "Free Silver" would have tended to increase inflation, Alanson's persistence on the strict "Gold Standard" would have been seen as the wrong solution today. Allowing "Free Silver" would have had the effect of increasing the money supply. This is similar to what we do today in lowering the prime rate offered by the Federal Reserve, thus increasing the amount of money available for investment. Of course, in Alanson's time there was no way to easily do the equivalent of raising the prime rate to stem inflationary pressures if that was needed later. Thus it would be somewhat unfair to judge his opinion on this issue by present day standards.[57]

Alanson gave his *Memorial Day Address* speech of May 30, 1889 (the Fox's had been in Detroit for just over a year at the time) in his hometown of Painted Post New York. Full of personal Civil War remembrances, this speech also showed Alanson's progressive side as he advocated for Blacks and for reconciliation with Confederate Soldiers as a way to maintain the still fragile union. His speech ended with:

> *Under the sod and the dew*
> *Awaiting the Judgment Day*
> *Under the one the Blue*
> *Under the other the Gray*[58]

The last speech we have illustrated Alanson's ties and beliefs associated with the Baptist church. *The Value of Early Investments, Remarks by A. J. Fox of Detroit before Baptist Home Mission Society at Saratoga Springs, May 30, 1895,* was by its nature more "evangelical" than any of the other talks. This speech dealt with the expansion of "Baptist Ideals" and he used his extensive business background to solicit donations for new churches in the West. Of course Alanson's zeal in the promotion of his religion, though probably common in the

Protestant dominated society of the time, seemed one-sided and paternalistic in today's light:

> *Schools are being founded among them as well as churches and the missionaries of this Society are looking after the moral, intellectual, and spiritual growth and seeking to develop among them a sprit of loyalty and patriotism, of reverence for the public schools, the American Flag and the Christian religion. Under the folds of this Triple banner of intelligence, patriotism and Christianity the Home Mission Society is pressing forward its work under (more) favorable auspices than ever before.[59]*

Alanson's speeches gave the impression that he was a fair, open-minded man, strong in his convictions yet respectful of others. He was probably quite progressive for his time. A self-educated man without a college education his talks showed he was well versed in Western history and literature (though with a distinct European/Christian slant). One example being when he retold the story of the origin of the word tariff:

> *The word Tariff we are told is derived from the name of a seaport in Southern Spain on the Mediterranean Sea, Tarifa. This port in older times was headquarters for the Moorish pirates who used to tally out from there and levy plunder from vessels passing through the Straits of Gibraltar.[60]*

How many Americans of today are versed in history enough to tell the following story taken from his *Memorial Day Address of 1889*:

> *Scottish poetry tells us of Lord James Douglass journeying with a band of Scottish knights to place the heart of King*

*Robert Bruce* (The Bruce of contemporary *Braveheart* fame) *in the Holy Sepulcher. As these soldier pilgrims were passing through Spain in the journey to Jerusalem they find the Christian King of that country at war with the Moors and a battle just imminent. Of course the Scotchmen volunteer to aid the Cross against the Crescent and are assigned a place of honor in the fight. The battle was hotly fought but the Muslims (?) were driven back before 'the long fell swoop of the Scottish blade' and victory rested on the banners of the Christian host. The Scotchmen had covered themselves with glory but their victory was dearly bought for Douglass was killed. The Spanish King mingled his tears and lamentations with those of the dead chieftains friends and was answered by a Scottish noblemen in words of dignity and pride which closed with these prophetic strains.*

*"But be then strong of heart Lord King*
*For this I tell thee sure*
*The sod that drank the Douglass blood*
*Shall never bear the Moor."*[61]

As shown by this last quote, and as was probably true of most American's of the time, Alanson had little knowledge or understanding of non-Western/non-Christian cultures, specifically those of the Middle East as well as the original inhabitants of the "New World." From his *Baptist Home Mission Society* speech:

*Along our Northern frontier and through Canada the early Jesuit Missionaries, with self sacrificing devotion almost unparalleled in the history of the world planted the banner of the cross from the Gulf of St. Lawrence to the Mississippi and the effect of their labors has never been wiped out. The Indians of the North West* (Michigan, Wisconsin, Minnesota) *so far as they have had any religion at all have been almost without exception Roman Catholics. Those missionary labors were not lost on them though they were the least susceptible of all people to religions impressions.*[62]

I don't think the Ojibwa who had called the area around Manistique home for hundreds of years before the Chicago Lumbering Company arrived would have agreed with this statement. It would have been interesting to know Alanson's thoughts when he sat in his library and read the newspaper accounts of the massacre at Wounded Knee on December 29, 1890.

As the 19th Century drew to a close Alanson found himself turning 67 years of age. Sixty-seven was a respectable age for a time still 40 years away from the widespread use of vaccines and more importantly antibiotics. As was usually the case prior to the second half of the 20th Century, viruses and bacteria were the great equalizers. For all Alanson's wealth, influence, and good fortune his life had not been without personal loss. He had lost his first wife Abigail 29 years earlier in 1871. His daughter Julia died in 1891 being only 22 years old. His son Stuart died in 1894 at 23. And his young son Joseph died in 1884 at the age of 5.

During his time there Alanson made an addition to the rear of the Ransom Gillis House. The bricks for this addition were of a slightly different hue making it obvious to the eye even today.[63] This addition is actually more evident today than it was in 1901 due to the landscaping present at the time. At the end of the 19th Century a walk down John R or Alfred streets was like a stroll though an Ivy League campus. The brick structures had ivy creeping up their external walls halting neatly at the beginning of their steep slate-tiled roofs. Large deciduous trees were present in the yards as well as on the easement between the street and the paved sidewalk. A low, highly detailed wrought iron fence surrounded each property. In the case of the Ransom Gillis House this fencing accented the design of the wrought iron of the Mansard roof atop the structure. All of this would have made the addition to the house barely noticeable at the time.[64]

On the first floor of the Ransom Gillis House there were two bays. One faced southwest towards John R and the other faced northeast. One of these bays was surely part of Alanson's great library. The bay facing towards John R had a fireplace at its center; it was the ideal place. You can just imagine him sitting at his desk in the winter, a warm fire glowing in the fireplace as he gazed out the window to see a light dusting of snow falling on his yard and the sidewalk facing John R. In the Spring the fire would be out and the windows would be open to allow a light breeze to enter.

While Alanson sat quietly in his library, two houses away at 77 Alfred Street resided a little fat boy of 7 named Russell McLauchlin. To Russell the environment on Alfred Street was held in a far different light, it was a "golden quarter-mile" full of the endless adventures and "splendors of a healthy, normal boyhood."[65, 66] In 1946 Russell, then a columnist for the Detroit News, wrote a book of compiled "reminisces" of his childhood entitled simply, "Alfred Street." This book was full of stories of the characteristics and characters on Alfred Street including popcorn vendors selling at a penny-a-bag, summer lemonade stands, childhood territorial alliances, summer nights on the front porch, and their takes on the local spinsters. One such story involved none other than Mary Stebbins, sister of Alanson's second wife Cornelia, who also resided with the Fox's at 63 Alfred Street. Russell in his book described her as:

> *Miss Stebbins lived just two doors away, in her married sister's household, and it was Miss Stebbins' fancy to get herself up like a Victorian belle and go flouncing down the street in what certainly resembled a hoop-skirt. She had a*

*deep voice and a manner so formidably aristocratic that*
*Freddy Morris called her family-circle by the overall title of*
*"the Stebbinses," although she was the only one of six who*
*bore that name.*[67]

To Russell the Alfred Street of his youth was a dream-like place, a place that is formed in the minds of all who have healthy childhoods. Places of which all that have the opportunity to experience it spend the rest of their life relishing. Mr. McLauchlin did the same and as such ended his book with the following:

> *How can you get to Alfred Street?*
> *I'll tell you, Ruth, in rhyme.*
> *Somehow or other, find a bus*
> *Marked "Once Upon a Time."*
> *And let it drop you at a place*
> *Where your own, eager feet*
> *Once walked the ways of childhood:*
> *And you'll be at Alfred Street!*[68]

By the late 1910's the breeze coming through Alanson's window had lost its fresh scent. The burgeoning industrial area at the shores of the Detroit River was encroaching upon the environs of Alfred Street. As these industrial facilities and the accommodations to house their employees expanded from the riverfront in the upcoming years, the Blue Bloods of Alfred Street started to flee. But at the closing of the 19th Century, life on this street and the surrounding area was the easiest it would ever be.

As Alanson was nearing the end of his life a new venture was going to begin on the property of 63 Alfred Street. In

1903 Mary Chase Perry was looking for a location to start her own pottery. During this search she noted that:

> *Automobiles were superceding carriages. Many stables were being vacated. Back of a well-known residence in an entirely desirable neighborhood on Alfred Street was an empty barn – just the place to start a small Pottery. I walked by it and around it before I had the courage to ring the bell of the Alanson Fox residence, and was ushered into the famous library where I found Mr. Fox.*[69]

Alanson was intrigued by Mary's proposal to turn his recently vacated carriage house into a pottery and after a short discussion they settled on a rent of eight dollars a month, an arrangement that continued for three years. After the pottery was up and running he would frequently pay a visit. Mary thought Mr. Fox was particularly interested in the new methods they were using there, specifically when her partner Horace Caulkins would melt scrap gold and silver that he had gotten from local dentists so that she could incorporate them into her glazes.[70]

In early October of 1903 Alanson made out his Last Will and Testament in preparation for a trip to New York City for medical treatment.[71] Unfortunately complications from this medical treatment set in and he died there on October 29, 1903 of blood poisoning (or toxemia, bacteria in the blood, as we would describe it today).[72,73,74] The following October, on the 12th through the 15th Mary Chase Perry held her first pottery exhibition from her newly formed Pewbic Pottery located in the stable behind the Ransom Gillis House. Alanson's widow Cornelia hosted this event for her society friends.[75]

Alanson's wife Cornelia and her sister Mary remained living at 63 Alfred Street for a short time, but with her husband gone she moved back to New York by 1906. She died in New York City many years later on March 14th 1929. She was

88 years old. Shortly after Cornelia left the house it was occupied by Mr. & Mrs. James Haines Drake. They never purchased the property and were gone within a few years. At this time the last "Blue Blood" family occupied the house, the family of Reverend Maurice Penfield Fikes. Maurice was the pastor at the Woodward Avenue Baptist Church, the same church in which Alanson was so heavily involved in while living in Detroit. The Fikes may have known the Fox's through their church. Maurice entered into a land contract to purchase the property on April 20th 1909. During their years in Detroit the Fikes split their time between 63 Alfred Street and a summer home in Long Lake, Michigan (near Traverse City). [76,77,78,79,80]

In 1910 the Reverend lived at 63 Alfred Street with his Wife, their three teenage children, a domestic servant, and a seamstress (presumably due to the fact that his two teenage daughters needed to be presentable to society). Seven people living in a house on this street had been the norm since the 1870's. Six houses down, still within the same block and on the same side of the street, there was now a Rooming House. Seventeen people from 11 separate families lived there.[81]

The onslaught of the proletariat had begun.

# Rooming House & Restaurant

*"Employees should use plenty of soap and water in the home, and upon their children, bathing frequently ... Nothing makes for right living and health so much as cleanliness. Notice that the most advanced people are the cleanest."*

*--- Helpful Hints and Advice to Employees:*
*To Help Them Grasp the Opportunities Which Are Presented to Them by the Ford*
*Profit-Sharing Plan,*
*Ford Motor Company, 1915[1]*

As Reverend Fikes settled into his position as pastor of the Woodward Avenue Baptist Church and his family into their new home I wonder whether they knew that the gilded age of Alfred Street was coming to an end. Theirs would be the last name listed in the Detroit Blue Books at the address of 63 Alfred Street. A rooming house had sprouted up only a few doors down the street, others would follow closely.

Just a few blocks away lived a 28-year-old woman from a very different background; their paths would soon cross. Bertha Noeske was the daughter of German immigrants who arrived in this country around 1870. Bertha did not fit into the mold of women of her mother's generation. Bertha was different, she wanted more, she was what we would call today an entrepreneur. In 1910 she was running a Rooming House, but she wanted to secure her future by purchasing a property of her own. She wanted to build wealth through property just like the immigrant Fox Family had over 200 years prior. Late in the 1910's Bertha started looking for an investment opportunity.[2,3]

Back at 63 Alfred Street the Fikes' started to have problems. As more and more houses on the street were accommodating boarders the aristocratic atmosphere waned. The congregation at the Woodward Avenue Baptist church surely reflected these demographic changes. Maybe these changes increased the stresses Reverend Fikes experienced at home. Whatever the specific causes by 1919 Maurice and his wife Mary of over 27 years were divorced. Maurice moved back East to Trenton Junction, New Jersey. Mary with her youngest daughter Nita moved into the Plaza Hotel just off Grand Circus Park in Downtown Detroit. Just three years after Reverend Fikes paid off the land contract on the Ransom Gillis House to Cornelia Fox, he himself sold the property to the enterprising Bertha Noeske. Bertha's mother Albertina co-signed on the purchase. Bertha and her mother assumed three mortgages on the property, two held by the Detroit Savings Bank and one to Maurice's wife Mary (part of the divorce settlement no doubt). In addition they assumed the lease of a boarder, Harry Vrooman, already staying at the house. It seems that even before Bertha purchased the property it was being occupied by renters. The Golden Age of Alfred Street had ended.[4,5,6]

By 1920 the structure at 63 Alfred Street had been fully converted to a rooming house. A house that once had been occupied by one family and two or three domestic servants now housed 35 people. The interior by then most certainly held little resemblance to its original configuration. The once stately rooms were divided up using whatever was available. Some of the renters had access to cooking facilities, but most probably did not. Even more critical would have been the bathroom facilities. Since additional plumbing for more bathrooms would have been cost prohibitive, the facilities were most certainly communal. One can only imagine the deplorable conditions that must have quickly developed. The families living there probably had first dibs on the best facilities. The roomers or lodgers probably had to make due with whatever was left, many of them just glad to have a place to stay. Residents probably slept in shifts orchestrated by their working hours, which industrialization had pushed to around the clock. As with many other similar houses in the city, louse-borne typhus and tuberculosis would have been rampant.[7,8,9] Even under what we would view today as Third World conditions, these poor and uneducated immigrants from Europe were much better off than they had been in their homelands. Back across the Atlantic crops imported from the New World (potatoes, maize, etc.) had helped facilitate a population explosion. With the amount of land static their living conditions degraded quickly. The poor saw the path to escape in America, a "vacant" landscape larger than they could imagine just calling to be "filled up."[10]

In 1900 over 100 of the City's well off were listed as living on Alfred Street in the society Blue Book of Detroit. By 1911 this number had been reduced to 47. In 1917 only 8 remained and these no doubt elderly holdouts of a by-gone era. Their compatriots were dead or had escaped to the suburbs and beyond.[11,12,13]

In what seems to be an effort to hamper our exploration of the legacy of the Ransom Gillis House, the older streets of Detroit were re-numbered effective January 1st, 1921. The actual motivation for this was to eliminate the addition of half numbers that was routinely occurring as plots on these older streets were divided up and the structures there in being converted to rooming houses. After this first day of 1921 the address of the Ransom Gillis House officially changed from 63 Alfred Street to 205 Alfred Street.[14]

The once Ivy covered stable that saw the origination of Pewbic Pottery passed through a number of incarnations after Mary Chase and her pottery moved out in 1906. It was an auto repair shop, battery service shop, and a filling station before it was torn down in 1935.[15,16] It was replaced by a new structure, a restaurant.[17] This coincided with the sale of the back of the property. A sale that was probably prompted by Bertha's struggle to keep the rooming house during the depression. The restaurant continued operation until the mid-1950's.

Eventually Bertha lost her battle to keep the property where Henry T. Brush's structure stood and the Detroit Savings Bank foreclosed on her in 1936.[18] But the life of this house was far from over. Soon another family would enter the picture, one that originated 6000 miles away in the heart of the Ottoman Empire.

## US Census 63 Alfred Street 1920[19]

| Name | | Sex | Age | Martial Status | Place of Birth | Occupation |
|---|---|---|---|---|---|---|
| Malta Vrooman | Head | F | 50 | D | Vermont | Head of household |
| Eloier Platz | Daughter | F | 20 | M | Michigan | None |
| Fred Platz | Son-in-Law | M | 21 | M | Michigan | Bookkeeper, Chemical Company |
| H. Vrooman | Son | M | 22 | S | Michigan | Elevator Operator |
| Luciler Tagnay | Lodger | M | 32 | S | Canada | Sales |
| Letta Cook | Lodger | F | 48 | D | Canada | Restaurant Cashier |
| Claudett Haydren | Lodger | F | 26 | W | Florida | None |
| Phyllis Haydren | Lodger | F | 8 | S | New York | None |
| ? Barrows | Lodger | F | 45 | W | Kansas | Trained Nurse |
| Mary Barrows | Lodger | F | 22 | S | Kansas | Trained Nurse |
| Charles Gates | Lodger | M | 35 | S | Michigan | Railroad Fireman |
| James Howe | Lodger | M | 40 | S | Ohio | Brick Mason |
| Francis Smith | Lodger | F | 21 | S | Michigan | Department Store Saleslady |
| Clara Pulaski | Lodger | F | 24 | S | Michigan | Telephone Operator |
| Mary Smith | Lodger | F | 27 | S | Michigan | Telephone Operator |
| Anna Smith | Lodger | F | 28 | S | Michigan | Factory Timekeeper |
| Manreia (?) Smith | Lodger | F | 17 | S | Michigan | Telephone Operator |
| Laura Tori | Lodger | F | 24 | S | Michigan | Telephone Operator |
| Sadia Tori | Lodger | F | 32 | S | Michigan | Restaurant Waitress |
| Manrie Douley | Lodger | F | 34 | S | Michigan | Trained Nurse |
| Mary Delmoncio | Lodger | F | 22 | M | New York | Hotel Checker |
| Thresa Freedman | Lodger | F | 24 | S | Ohio | Telephone Operator |
| Paul Milnarch | Head | M | 25 | M | Hungaria | Machine Operator |
| Mary Milnarch | Wife | F | 18 | M | Hungaria | None |
| Frank Morrison | Head | M | 32 | M | New York | Manufacturing Company Polisher |
| Beatrise Morrison | Wife | F | 31 | M | New York | None |
| Raxnor Morrison | Son | M | 10 | S | New York | Son |
| Herbert Maxwell | Head | M | 38 | M | New York | Theater (?) |
| Mary Maxwell | Wife | F | 38 | M | Michigan | Hotel Checker |
| Walter Davis | Head | M | 40 | M | Louisiana | Shop Plumber |
| Dora Davis | Wife | F | 25 | M | Minnesota | (?) Swing |
| Alfred J. Murphy | Head | M | 52 | M | Michigan | General Practice lawyer |
| Margret Murphy | Wife | F | 45 | M | Michigan | None |
| Margret Murphy | Daughter | F | 14 | S | Michigan | None |
| (?) Giboney | Servant | F | 60 | S | Michigan | Private Family Servant |

Total Occupants 35

# US Census 63 (205) Alfred Street 1930[20]

| Name | | Sex | Age | Marital Status | Place of Birth | Occupation |
|---|---|---|---|---|---|---|
| Andrew Rich | Head | M | 47 | M | Canada | Manager Rooming House |
| Eva Rich | Wife | F | 40 | M | Canada | Housekeeper Rooming House |
| Velma Rich | Daughter | F | 16 | S | Canada | None |
| Madeline Rich | Daughter | F | 10 | S | Canada | None |
| Walter Grolie | Roomer | M | 36 | S | Switzerland | Foundry Blacksmith |
| Howard Ballen | Roomer | M | 39 | S | Michigan | Auto Factory Laborer |
| Sarah Kirven | Roomer | F | 69 | D | Canada | None |
| John Myers | Roomer | M | 41 | S | Michigan | Real Estate Salesman |
| Mary Anitiony | Roomer | F | 33 | S | Michigan (Syrian) | Auto factory Mfg. (?) |
| Les Anitiony | Roomer | M | 24 | S | Michigan (Syrian) | Auto factory laborer |
| Frank Elais | Roomer | M | 28 | M | Syria | Shoe repair, shoemaker |
| Conrado Gergman | Head | M | 34 | M | Philippines | Auto factory merchant |
| Mable Gergman | Wife | F | 30 | M | New York | Club housework |
| John Gordon | Head | M | | M | US | |
| Mary Gordon | Wife | F | | M | US | |
| Leand Shaw | Roomer | M | 28 | M | Afghanistan | Auto factory polisher |
| Henry Fukalek | Head | M | 43 | M | Michigan | Auto factory (?) |
| Mae Fukalek | Wife | F | 39 | M | Missouri | Restaurant waitress |
| Laura Boulware | Daughter | F | 13 | S | Missouri | None |
| Guy Franklen | Head | M | 28 | M | California | Restaurant Chef |
| Joan Franklen | Wife | F | 23 | M | Michigan | Restaurant Waitress |
| Arthur Wallace | Head | M | 39 | M | Penn. | Tailor shop, tailor |
| Odelle Wallace | Wife | F | 27 | M | Alabama | None |
| Betty Wallace | Daughter | F | 1 | S | Michigan | None |

Total Occupants 24

# The Essa's

*"Alfred Street still exists. It runs at right angles to Woodward Avenue, less than a mile from the center of Detroit, just as it always did. It is now in what city-planners call a blighted area. The elms were long ago cut down.[a] No representative of the old neighbor-families remains. The houses, mostly standing as they stood a half-century ago, are dismal structures. Some have night-blooming grocery stores in their front yards. Some have boarded windows. All stand in bitter need of paint and repair.*

*It is a desolate street; a scene of poverty and chop-fallen gloom; possibly of worse things."*

*--From Alfred Street, by Russell McLauchlin, 1946*

George Essa laid face down in the fertile black soil of the Cilician Plain outside the city of Adana in the heart of the Ottoman Empire.[b] The soil around him was moist, but it was not from rain, it was from the blood of the dead and dying in his midst. He dared not move, he dared not even breathe as it might betray to his tormentors that he was actually still alive. Turks and Kurds, some he had been friendly with just a few months before, were hacking at those around him as if they were cattle. Some of those who now laid about him had begged their oppressors to simply shoot them in the head but they "answered that cartridges cost money and they did not propose to waste money on Christians."[1] The adults pleaded with them as the sounds of their children moaning in pain, crying out for their parents, was a hell far worse than anything Lucifer could ever conjure up. "Please let them die quickly and fall into God's hands," they begged, but this was to no avail, their once amiable neighbors could not hear, their senses were numbed by the racial and religious fervor they had been swept up in. To them the beings upon which their swords fell were not human, if they allowed themselves to consider them

---

[a] The elms were long cut down to make room for widening of the street to accommodate flow and parking.
[b] Located in the SE corner of present day Turkey.

human they could not stomach what they were doing. They showed no empathy for their victims. All they felt was rage.[2,3,4,5]

Those with swords and those on the ground were really not that different from one another genetically; actually by today's standards they were quite similar. There was one defining difference though; those on the ground were Christians and those killing them were Muslims. It was April of 1909, some 30 miles to the south lay the beautiful turquoise waters of the Eastern Mediterranean, it should have been a very pleasant time of the year. Yet for months now the whole Ottoman Empire had been thrust into changes that would quickly culminate in its dissolution. After 600 years of existence, the Empire was in its last throws. It had only been held together in the prior 30 by the political adeptness of its Sultan, Abdul Hamid II. The Empire's failure to modernize along with its corrupt and inept bureaucracy made it impossible to respond to changes occurring in the rest of Europe. Consequently every year found it falling further and further in debt and losing more and more of its territory. The Sultan had used various methods to hold his crumbling empire together, not the least of which was the age-old ethnic and religious differences between the majority Muslims and the minority Armenians.[6,7]

In 1908 a mainly secular group called the Young Turks took power from the Sultan in a bloodless coup. This change of power was a bright light for the minorities throughout the Ottoman Empire, as they saw it as a lifting of the oppression so prevalent under Abdul Hamid II. When they took power the Young Turks announced a *Proclamation for the Ottoman Empire, 1908,* item 10 said:

> *The free exercise of the religious privileges which have been accorded to different nationalities will remain intact.*[8]

This proclamation by the Young Turks brought optimism to the minorities throughout the Empire including the Armenians, as well as other Christians, and the Jews. They hoped this would bring back the freedom they had steadily lost under the Sultan. [9] A small number of Armenians took this newfound freedom to the next level and started political activity (hardline Muslims would come to call this agitation). Some extremists even envisioned the reestablishment of an independent Armenian state within the Ottoman territories, something that had not existed for over 600 years. [10] These partisans and their supporters, both secular and religious, started arming themselves (something forbidden under the Sultan). The Armenians saw this armament as a way to protect their rights; the Turks saw this as preparations for civil war. For the most part, these Armenian militiamen were small in number and no real threat to the central government, but their rhetoric would be used as a tool to galvanize opposition to the Armenian population as a whole. [11,12,13,14]

Many Muslims initially welcomed the government of the Young Turks as they viewed Abdul Hamid's authoritarian rule as a major reason why the Ottoman's were losing their dominance in the world. [15] For a few months the outlook was very positive, but 600 years of Turkish bureaucracy and tradition could not be transformed in such a short period of time. Under this weight the empire's collapse was inevitable. The Young Turks simply did not have enough time. Across the Bosporus the Ottoman territories in southeastern Europe were gaining their independence from the Empire and the Young Turks could do nothing. The Muslim majority envisioned even their dominant position in the homeland eroding as the Armenians as well as other minorities were gaining new political rights. These issues only increased the Turkish population's feeling of inferiority and quickly weakened support for the new government. Abdul Hamid II, ousted less than a year earlier, saw in these developments a path back to power. The ex-Sultan and his loyalists took full advantage of this situation. In the Armenians, the Sultan found the spark to ignite the social prejudices of the majority and use them to reestablish his power. He used his population's current self-loathing and unified them behind a "common" and "convenient" enemy.[16,17,18,19]

It did not help that the European powers were not simply standing by silently while these events were unfolding. Unfortunately, the Armenians were situated between Russia and their long time desire for a warm water port on either the Mediterranean Sea or the Persian Gulf. There were rumors that the Russians were supplying support to the Armenian partisans in order to improve their chances of acquiring this port as the Empire continued to crumble. Whether truthful or not, it only added to the indignation of the Muslims. Complicating issues even further were the English and French who were dead set against Russia obtaining its' warm water port.[20]

The conditions were ripe for a racial catastrophe.

All this political intrigue was unknown to George Essa; all he knew was that he needed to stay very, very still, hopefully the Muslims butchering those around him would think he was already dead. His tormentors built bonfires out of wood and hay and started tossing bodies, some still living, into the flames. He was able to withstand the screams and moans of those dying around him as being only 19 his youthful, testosterone laden body allowed him to maintain his concentration on the job at hand, keeping perfectly still.[21] Eventually the Muslim's rage subsided and they left, luckily for George leaving many of the bodies to rot in the field. George remained there among the stench of rotting flesh for two more days, until he felt it was safe enough to get up.[22]

Though the majority of people in the field that day with George Essa were Armenians, he himself was not. He had lived his entire life on the Cilician Plain near Adana but he was a Chaldean not an Armenian. An ancient race, a sect of

Assyrians, the Chaldeans could trace their history back to before 600 BC.[23] George spoke many languages reflecting the diverse population that existed in what would eventually become eastern Turkey. He spoke Kurdish, Arabic, Turkish, among others, but his native tongue was Chaldean, a modern version of Aramaic, the language used in the Holy Land at the time of Christ. Chaldean's were fond of noting that theirs was the "language of Christ."[24] The Chaldeans were one of the first converted to Christianity, even before the Armenians some would say, and that conversion almost two millennia before was what had placed George in the field that day. Although the local Turk's rage was directed towards their misplaced fear of the Armenian presence, George being a Christian (Catholic to be exact) was lumped in with them. The scythe of racial and religious hatred cuts a wide swath and George had been caught up in it. As he stood up and brushed the dirt from his clothes his first thought was to wash the stench of death off him. He, along with his brothers Tom and John, knew it was time to leave and they knew exactly where they wanted to escape to, America. The question was how? It would take them a few years to accomplish this task and their route would not be a direct one, but they soon found themselves in Detroit and eventually would add their stories to all the others that had passed through the house on the corner of Alfred Street and John R.

The path to America for George and his brothers Tom and John was not an easy one. After the massacre at Adana the Essa brothers made their way to Tel Kaif[c] in present day Iraq. They were welcomed there, as this village had been occupied by Assyrians for over 2000 years. Tel Kaif was a suburb of Nineveh of antiquity, now present day Mosul. There John Essa married a local Chaldean Amina in the house of her

---

[c] Tel Kaif is the Arabic spelling, English it is spelled Tel Keppe, in Syriac (Eastern Aramaic) it is spelled Tel Keipeh

parents. Even though one of the largest populations of Chaldeans in the area lived in Tel Kaif, the town was still dominated by Muslims, mainly Kurds but also Arabs. As with most of the other areas of the crumbling Ottoman Empire at the time, Christians were still looked upon with suspicion in Tel Kaif. For this reason John's marriage was conducted in his wife's parents living room. A ceremony in a public church at that time would not have been safe. Soon after, the Essa brothers acted on their plans to leave the oppression they had experienced all their lives. Unfortunately in the early 1910's immigration to the US was, as it had been for some 30 years, dominated by Europeans primarily from Germany. George, Tom, John, and his new wife Amina could not obtain visas to enter the United States. But escape from the Ottoman's was a must. John and Amina were able to obtain visas to immigrate to Mexico, settling in the town of San Luis Potosi. There John continued to make a living in the trade that had been taught to him by his father, leather working and shoe making. To this day there still is a Chaldean population in the San Luis Potosi area.[25,26]

Tom and George could not follow their brother and his new wife to Mexico; but they were able to obtain visas for Canada. Tom and George in their flight from Tel Kaif first traveled to Beirut. The cosmopolitan nature of that city easily allowed them to find passage through the Mediterranean to Liverpool where ships across the Atlantic were numerous. Even though the trip from Beirut to the New World would be the longest, this was not the most difficult. They first had to make it across the Syrian Desert. There they had to find passage with the Bedouin, the ancient nomadic herders of the Middle East. Tom and George were not comfortable in the desert, as they had grown up in the fertile plain around Adana. They were most apprehensive about this part of their journey. Halfway across the desert the brothers came to the oasis at the town of Tadmur. There they took a rest from the oppressive heat. Just outside of the small village was the ancient Roman ruins of Palmyra. As Tom and George walked through these ruins they talked among themselves wondering who had built such marvelous structures, what had become of their builders, and why they had been allowed to crumble. Little did they know that they were soon to be involved with a structure thousands of miles away in Detroit. A structure which at the dawning of the 21$^{st}$ century people would be asking the same questions of. But their interest in Palmyra only lasted a short time, they had to move on. Leaving Tadmur and the ruins of Palmyra, they headed back out into the desert on their way to the coast. Soon their luck ran out and they fell victims to Bedouin bandits who took all they had. Even though, they still arrived at the Mediterranean, made their way to Liverpool where they found passage across the Atlantic. Upon their arrival in Canada they settled in Fort William, Ontario[d] and awaited an opportunity to travel to the United States and be reunited with their brother John. [27,28,29]

As the Fikes' marriage was disintegrating under the pressures of the transitioning neighborhood on Alfred Street and Bertha Noeske was dreaming of buying some property for herself, Tom and George continued to attempt to get their visas to emigrate from Canada to the United States. George obtained his first arriving in Detroit in 1916. Four years later Tom followed him.[30,31] There they were reunited with John and Amina who had recently arrived in Detroit from San Luis Potosi. None of the Essas had very much education past grade school, but they brought with them two invaluable assets; they were White[e] and Christian. This combination of religion and ethnicity that had been such a liability in Adana and Tel Kaif would be turned on its end. In America these traits allowed them to assimilate seamlessly into this new culture. The

---

[d] Now Thunder Bay, Ontario

[e] Very White as a matter of fact, hailing from an area close to the Caucasus Mountains from which the term Caucasian is derived.

United States had always been a predominantly Protestant country ever since the first European immigrants, the Fox's among them, arrived from England in the 1600's. The Essa's Catholic version of Christianity was not much of a liability (as it was in other areas of the US) in Detroit, as the city still retained some of the vestiges of the original French settlers in 1701. Catholicism in Detroit was to grow even more dominant in the ensuing 30 years as the city attracted many Polish and Slavic immigrants from Eastern Europe. They brought with them their devout Catholic beliefs. Ironically, upon their arrival in the United States the Essa brothers were required to register for military service in WWI. This would have sent them right back across the Atlantic to battle against the oppressors from which they had just fled.[32,33]

In 1914 Henry Ford, in an effort to stem incessant turnover plaguing all the companies in the burgeoning auto industry, established his famous Five-Dollar-a-Day program. The continually increasing dependence on the assembly line in these plants was foreign and difficult for people to adapt to, especially those from a rural/farming background. Workers in these plants found serving machines particularly tedious and demeaning. The result was careers of employees measured in months or even days instead of years. The Essa boys were perfectly suited to Henry Ford's ideal of a reliable, long-time, worker, whom he rewarded with an income significantly higher than similar jobs at other auto manufacturers. Compared to life in the Middle East, Detroit was a paradise to the Chaldeans. They did not mind the hard work and their family life easily met the requirements of the Ford Motor Company's Sociological Department which oversaw employees "suitability" for Five-Dollars-a-Day. Soon George was working at Ford, a proud member of the Five-Dollars-a-Day workforce.[34,35,36,37]

John and Amina upon coming to Detroit left the leather working trade behind them in Mexico. With only grade school educations they both had to find a new way to make a living. Initially they struggled spending some time on public assistance. To their benefit the Chaldean community in Detroit was growing at the time and, as with many new immigrant populations, they supported one another by congregating around their faith. A faith that now they could practice out in the open without threat of reprisals. Eventually they centered on St. Maron's Catholic Church on Congress Street in downtown Detroit. Detroit has remained a hub for Chaldeans up to the present day, with over 30,000 living in the state, primarily in the Detroit Metro area.[38,39,40]

John Essa eventually started selling Dry Goods[f] door to door.[41] Interestingly enough he may have bought some of his products wholesale from the dry goods house of Edison, Moore & Company of which Gaylord Wilson Gillis was a member like his father Ransom before him. By this time though the Gillis family had long made their exit from Alfred Street, settling like many others of their ilk in the affluent northeast suburb of Grosse Point.[42,43]

By 1938 John Essa was already 56 years old. He and his family had been in Detroit for over 20 years and door-to-door sales were wearing him down, it was time to make a change. His eldest child Ann had found a rooming house recently foreclosed on by The Detroit Bank. She was thinking of leasing it and adding a small grocery store in the front lot. John's brother Tom was already running a small grocery in the city.[44] The house she was interested in was none other than the Ransom Gillis House at the corner of John R and Alfred. There were Chaldeans in that area of town and even a few boarders in the house itself by 1930.[g,45] A few years earlier Bertha Noeske had lost the house she had bought together with

---

[f] Usually Dry Goods are in reference to fabric, clothing, etc., as opposed to groceries and hardware.

[g] In 1930 Census documents in Detroit many Chaldeans, Tom Essa being one of them, were noted as Syrians by the Enumerator (census taker) walking house to house.

her mother, defaulting on the mortgage to The Detroit Bank. All the buildings on Alfred Street had long been converted to rooming houses by this time and many had fallen in to disrepair. The upkeep of these massive 19th Century structures was extensive and nearly impossible under the economic conditions of the Depression. Yet the thick red brick walls of the Ransom Gillis House were empowered to withstand a significant amount of neglect.[46]

The 23-year-old Ann leased the house and asked her Father to help her add a storefront to the southwest corner. The walls of this new addition began in about the middle of the front of the house and about the same distance from the turret on the John R side. In order to facilitate the support of the roof beams for this addition, large notches were chiseled out of the exterior brick walls that were placed there so carefully some 60 years earlier. The windows directly under the turret and one on the Alfred Street side were filled with concrete. This allowed the existing wall to better support the added load of the new roof beams. Most disturbing was the modifications to the turret and its ornate support post. This post was now located inside the new storefront. The store was already going to be small, there was definitely no reason to have that post and its massive base taking up half the floor space, it had to go. It was removed, along with a good portion of the front porch, to make more room in the store. The turret now relied on the roof of the new store front for its only support. The ornate support post was removed just above of its beautiful Gothic capital and lost forever. The bottom portion of the turret was incorporated into the roof of the store front just below the quadruplets of flower blossoms. Tar from the roofing material was spread onto this lower portion of the turret to incorporate it into the new roof and keep out the extremes of Southeastern Michigan weather. Years later when the store front was demolished the turret lost its only support, causing it to eventually pull away from the main structure.[47,48,49]

Ann was the oldest and only girl born to John and Amina. The other four children were the boys Frank, Louie, Ernie, and Joe. As the 40's arrived so did WWII and all four of John Essa's boys served. Four left Detroit but only three returned. Joe died in the Pacific at Luzon.[50]

The brothers Tom, John, and George and their growing families stayed close in Detroit. One of George's sons remembers working stocking shelves at the grocery across the street from the one owned by his Uncle John and worrying that he might be seen "working for the competition." John Essa's young sons and their cousins also relished the opportunity to go down in the basement of the Ransom Gillis House with their BB guns to reduce the population of rats therein whenever the Health Department complained. Though the neighborhood had changed significantly since Russell McLauchlin was a kid there 40 years prior, the children there still found ways to amuse themselves as they do everywhere.[51]

Russell McLauchlin grew up on Alfred Street at the close of the 19th Century, just two structures down from the Ransom Gillis House, when it was owned by Alanson Fox. Russell remained in Detroit and by the 1940's was a columnist for the Detroit News. In 1944 he and some of his colleagues wrote a series of articles that reminisced about the gilded life on Alfred Street at the turn of the century and lamented the current "faded grandeur" of the area. But Mr. McLauchlin remembered his life there through the nostalgic gaze of youth. His "chop-fallen gloom" of Alfred Street in the 1940's was far from the impression of that street to the Essa's. For the Essa's this was the land of opportunity, a far cry from Adana and Tel Kaif. Sure they worked hard, probably harder than they should have, they were not rich by any means, but they treasured the freedoms they had never experienced before. Best of all, their children and grandchildren were given opportunities they themselves could have never imagined. So great would these opportunities be that within a few generations all knowledge of the Essa's life in the Middle East would become like a fictional tale of a far off land.[52,53]

Ann ran the store for four years then, at the age of 60, John Essa decided it was time to purchase the store and boarding house. He was too old for selling door to door. In May of 1942 John and his wife Amina purchased the Ransom Gillis Home with its attached storefront. The restaurant behind the house, built in 1935,[54] was not part of the transaction. The neighborhood around Alfred Street had been changing over the last ten years. It was located on the southwest boarder of what was then labeled Black Bottom, one of the few crowded areas were Detroit Blacks were "allowed" to live.[55] As in 1863, the great influx of unskilled workers from Europe and the cyclic nature of economics in the City, caused an escalation of tensions between the Blacks and Whites as they competed for the same finite resources.[56,57,58]

Black Bottom and the related Paradise Valley area were the primary locations in which Blacks were confined to in the City at the time. This limitation of Black housing areas was primarily enforced by protests and harassment of any of those who dared to move out into the predominantly White areas. As the population of this limited area increased the living conditions in Black Bottom and Paradise Valley fell as rents rose.[59,60]

There had always been racial tensions between Blacks and Whites in the City, normally the result of competition for jobs and living space. The Blacks, being the minority, usually came out on the losing end. Deep-seated prejudice prevailed among Whites from Northern as well as Southern origins. Some of these resulted in headline stories that gripped the attention of Detroit as well as the Nation. The Black Legion was one such case. An informal off shoot of the Ku Klux Klan with leaders originally from the South, the Black Legion claimed a membership of 10,000 in Wayne County. Many of these members were employed at local auto plants, local city governments, and most frighteningly local police departments. Among the murders attached to this group in the late 1930's was one of a Black man named Silas Coleman in a swamp near Pinckney Michigan. The motivation for this killing according to the perpetrators themselves was "to see what it feels like to shoot a Negro."[61] The specific influence of the Black Legion was short-lived in Detroit though as their racial rhetoric against Blacks was accompanied with oppositions to Catholics. This did not endear them to the majority of the White population in Detroit, over 70% of which were practicing Catholics.[62]

As workers flooded to Detroit in the early 1940's to support war production plants, the housing crisis quickly reached untenable proportions. Federally funded housing projects were initiated for White and Black workers. The problem quickly arose on where to locate the Black projects. There was no appropriate land available in the overcrowded traditionally Black areas so these new projects had to be built in predominately White neighborhoods. This quickly brought resistance from Whites who feared the projects would jeopardize their tenuous hold on home ownership. On the corner of Alfred and John R such pressures were not present. Since all the structures on the block had been boarding houses for over 20 years, those living in them had little concern with long-term property values. To their owners, these buildings were merely 'investments' and as such had lost any emotional component.[63]

Just prior to the Essa's purchase of the property in 1942, the social and housing pressures of war-time reached their breaking point about 7 miles to the northwest. The prior year a defense housing project, named Sojourner Truth,[h] had been completed and was (after some controversy) designated

<hr>

[h] After the Civil War era campaigner against slavery and for women's rights.

for Black families.  In the winter of that year opposition from the project's White neighbors began to escalate.  By February a sign was posted in the snow just outside the development, proudly sporting two small American flags on each end, as it proclaimed:

*WE WANT WHITE TENANTS IN OUR WHITE COMMUNITY* [64]

As the first Black families prepared to move into these new modest homes, they were met by a White mob.  This mob eventually swelled to over 1200 persons "armed with knives, clubs, rifles and shotguns, ready to do battle in the street separating the project from a row of dwellings occupied by white persons."  The protesters greatly outnumbered the police officers that were attempting to secure passage of these new Black residents.  After three barrages of tear gas fired into the crowd failed to facilitate their dispersal, the officer's efforts were deemed in vain and they and their charges turned away.[65]

George Essa sat at the counter of his brother John's store in front of 205 Alfred Street and combed over the Press coverage of the riots at the Sojourner Truth Project.  Everyone in Detroit was talking about it, with ones opinions usually braking down along racial lines.  George just sat there looking at the AP photo of police firing tear gas into the mob of White protesters.[66] When asked for his opinion he remained quiet, showing no emotion though his face seemed slightly flushed. Although he knew many languages, English was his last to acquire and thus his weakest.  Someone offered to read him the details of the story, he silently shook his head, No.  You see, George did not need to read the story; all he had to do was look at the picture.  The expressions on the faces of the angry White protesters he had seen before.  As a matter of fact, they were burned into his mind so that he could never forget no matter how hard he tried.  They were the same expressions of those who stood over him, swords and scythes in hand, in that field on the Cilician Plain some 33 years before.

After a month of negotiation and the assistance of 800 members of the Michigan National guard, Blacks were finally allowed access to their new homes in Sojourner Truth. The White resistance faded to about 250 protesters, mostly women, many pushing babies in their strollers, shouting and heckling officers as they gently broke up their picket line to allow the new tenants to pass. One wonders how these mothers explained their actions to these children years later.[67]

This by no means had mitigated the problem; it was merely a precursor of what was to come. In June of 1943, only a year after John Essa and his wife purchased the house and store at the corner of John R and Alfred Street, a full-blown riot broke out. A block to the West of the house on Woodward Avenue Whites were stopping trolleys pulling off the Blacks inside and beating them.[68,69] Four blocks East along the main Black business district of Hastings Street[i], almost all the businesses were vandalized by looters. By the end of the riot there were 34 dead and over 1800 arrested. Blacks numbered 25 of the dead and over 85% of those arrested.[70,71,72]

As Detroit moved into the mid-1950's the middle-class Whites' hold on their single-family homes outside the central city was as tenuous as ever. Since its origins with Henry Ford and his counterparts at the dawn of the 20th Century, Detroit's auto industry had been boom or bust. In bust times it was left to chronically inadequate city social services to pick up the pieces as best they could. The worst problems normally showed up as substandard housing for thousands of poor and minorities. As Blacks economically entered the middle class they wanted to leave the segregated confines and poor living conditions of Paradise Valley and Black Bottom. Moving out-

---

[i] Run us under a number of years later eliminating the heart of the Black community by the construction of I-75.

ward into the predominantly White neighborhoods Blacks met resistance on a grand and organized scale. Grassroots organizations in the form of homeowners associations became a dominant force in Detroit politics. These organizations were built upon the prejudicial fear that a Black influx would bring a myriad of social ills to the neighborhood. In reality the reaction by Whites in these neighborhoods was less a reflection of their fear of Blacks, but actually a result of their own insecurity in their ability to remain employed in the continually volatile automobile market.[73]

In a development eerily similar to the Mulas agitating the population in Adana 40 years earlier, pastors at Catholic churches actively encouraged their parishioners to participate in the formation of these homeowners associations. These pastors feared the influx of traditionally Protestant Blacks could jeopardize the close nit community upon which their parishes were built. In some cases these homeowners associations were actually formed around communities associated with a church rather than a specific neighborhood. Many of their meetings were held in parish buildings with full support of the pastor.[74]

The Essa brothers again found themselves in the middle. In Adana they were caught up in a conflict between the majority Turks and the minority Armenians. Then their race and religion had thrown them in with the minority, with tragic results. In Detroit they were lumped in with the majority by means of their Catholic faith and the color of their skin. The basic causes for the conflicts in Adana and Detroit were more similar than people would like to admit. In both cases the majority population was insecure about the future, and succumbed to the need to find a scapegoat to explain changes occurring around them of which they had no control. The magnitudes of these two conflicts were much different though. Individually tragic as these events were, the overall results were far less devastating in Detroit as they had been in Adana. In the Ottoman Empire during the last decades of its existence, the entire government structure and economy was collapsing. These ills were so widespread that the government of the Young Turks, no matter how well intentioned, had no means (or motivation) to halt the guttural response of the populous. The economic and social upheavals in Detroit (and other American cities) in the 1950's were a significant, but not an overwhelming situation for the US government to mitigate. The United States at the time was still a young and maturing economy with vast amounts of resources to draw upon. There were people and resources in far away locations of the country that did not have an emotional attachment to the events occurring in Detroit. Thus, these resources were quasi-neutral and could be used on both sides of the conflict to limit the consequences of violence simmering in the City. As a result, even though local governments in cities like Detroit could do little to stem this racial conflict, state and primarily Federal portions of the government could inject resources (as a last resort in the form of military troops) to keep the situation from descending into genocide. This is not to say that these State and Federal resources treated both sides of the conflict with an even hand, in most cases they did not[j,75], but they were able and willing to do much more to limit the bloodshed than the troops the Young Turks sent to Adana in 1909. There was also the availability of cheap and abundant land just outside the City limits that allowed Whites the option to flee instead of stay and fight.

As the 1950's gave way to the 1960's many State and Federal courts handed down rulings enforcing the rights of Blacks to purchase property anywhere they liked.[76] This could have lessened the housing pressures in the Black neighborhoods of Paradise Valley and Black Bottom if it were not for the concerted efforts of White Detroiters to find other means to keep their blocks "pure." These methods moved away from

---

[j] Even stories from the New York Times showed a distinct White bias not only in the reporting but also in the actions of the police.

intimidation, that was obviously illegal and to which the government could no longer turn a blind eye, to more subtle means. The new methods centered on access to the houses in the first place via real estate agents and restrictive covenants. The restrictive covenants basically did not allow homeowners to sell their homes to certain groups of people. These restrictive covenants were the first to be held unenforceable by the courts.[77] After these tactics failed Whites turned to the use of powers held by lenders and real estate agents.

Real estate agents enforced segregation by limiting the people who had access to the houses they put on the market. Michigan soon enacted laws and administrative rules to eliminate such practices.[k] Of course real estate associations were quite opposed to these restrictions and fought them in court.[78] The main argument of these realtors was that people should have the right to sell their property to whoever they please and that the agents are bound only to serve the requests of their customers. As Everett R. Trebilcock counsel for the Michigan Real Estate Association put it in 1962:

> *Real estate brokers must make it clear that they as agents have neither the right nor the duty to determine the racial, creedal or ethnic composition of any neighborhood.*
> *[The real objective of such legislation] is the attainment of open-occupancy housing by denying the real estate broker the right to serve property owners who are unwilling to dispose of their property [to minority groups]*[79]

But many Real Estate agents in Detroit had their actual motivations in pure profit, not their "right to serve property owners." In a tactic called 'Block Busting,' agents would use the fact or potential of Blacks moving into an all White neighbor-

---

[k] President Kennedy also considered a Federal Administrative Rule that would have had the same effect in late 1962.

hood to panic the homeowners into selling at 'rock-bottom' prices. In the meantime, these same agents were courting middle-class Blacks from the overcrowded and substandard housing of the central city. They were eager to pay a premium just for the opportunity to live outside the slums.[80]

The years of housing segregation in Detroit[l] had produced de facto segregation of the City's education system based on local neighborhood schools. Not only did the Black areas concentrate poverty, and the related social frustration and crime that accompanied it, but also their schools were underfunded which threatened to condemn future generations to the same fate.[81]

Meanwhile back on Alfred Street the results of continued housing discrimination since WWII took its toll. As overcrowding increased in Black Bottom and Paradise Valley so did all the social ills associated with it. This was intensified as the more affluent Blacks left the confines of these poverty-stricken neighborhoods. As Alfred Street fell further and further into poverty the crime in the area grew. At their Alfred John R Market, John Essa, and later in the 1960's his children, manned the register with a gun under the counter for protection. They also carried a gun with them as they left late at night to walk to their car to drive home. Iron bars that were once used as decorative elements on the roofs and fences enclosing neatly kept yards, were by this time installed on windows to dissuade would be break-ins overnight. Many of the owners of other small markets in the area simply gave up and closed their doors. John Essa's children hung onto their store into the 1960's.

As the other stores closed the Alfred John R Market stayed open because neighborhood people still needed to buy food. For a time their business actually increased due to these

---

[l] Even at the start of the 21st Century, the Detroit Metro area is one of the most segregated in terms of housing in the nation.

closings. Eventually though as the 1960's drew on it became too much and the Essas abandoned the store and boarding house. From that time on the building was never occupied again except for the occasional transient or drug dealer.[82]

Like many other Whites, John and Amina soon left Detroit and eventually settled for a time in the suburb of Westland. On January 9th 1973, a number of years after they had abandoned the house and store, John and his wife put their shaky signatures on a Quit Claim Deed selling the property to the Woodward East Project, Inc. As they signed this document in the witness of their sons Frank and Ernie one wonders whether they realized that they had come full circle. From being minorities under the persecution of the Ottoman Turks for their religion over 70 years prior to being in the majority in the racial struggles between Blacks and Whites in Detroit. Unlike the Ottoman Empire though, Detroit had a built in safety valve to relieve the accumulating social pressure. Whites in the Detroit area had the option of flight to the suburbs, allowing them to literally change the world in which they lived by simply driving a few minutes further up the expressway.[83]

The child of Henry T. Brush was now truly alone. Hiding in plain sight, keeping company only with those lacking the economic or educational means to leave.

# Urban Renewal?

*"We, the residents living within Mack and Gratiot, Woodward and Chrysler, combining our efforts for the purpose of promoting a greater sense of cooperation among and between us, having a voice in all civic matters affecting our community, maintaining and improving our property, and developing a sense of individual obligation in the area in which we reside."*

--Mission Statement, Woodward East Project, Inc., 1969[1]

When the Essa's came to Detroit in the late 1910's you could take electric streetcars to most anywhere inside the city. These light rail systems (electric interurbans as they were called at the time) reached as far north as Port Huron. Though these extensive light rail systems (mostly private) had been in operation since the 1890's and their predecessors, horse drawn streetcars, had been operating in Detroit since the 1850's, these modes of transportation were quickly becoming unprofitable. Despite the longstanding assumption that this decline was facilitated by a conspired effort of GM, Mack, Standard Oil, Firestone, and others that would stand to gain from the demise of mass transit, the truth was more likely that people favored the convenience and flexibility of cars. In 1916, long before the above conspiracy was supposedly hatched, the US congress passed the first act that provided matching funds to states for the building and maintenance of roads. Once the state and federal governments took more interest in road construction, their quality increased rapidly making the use of cars and buses far more practical. The state of Michigan soon established a gas tax and auto licensing fees to further support the construction of modern roads. In 1924 the State of Michigan recorded the nation's largest distance of new roads facilitated by the assistance of federal moneys. With the advent of all these new roads bus companies flourished in the 1920's, so much so that competition for passengers became fierce. Not only where buses more flexible, but more importantly the capital required to initiate them was a fraction of that of a train on rails. Buses simply did not have to provide their own right-of-way and maintain the tracks there in. They just used the public streets, most of which ran along side or on both sides of the existing transit rails. The bus companies could duplicate the train routes, arriving a few minutes prior and thus stealing the passengers waiting there. The glory days of rail-based rapid transit in the Detroit area were short-lived. In reality rail never had a chance, not because of greedy, all-powerful corporate giants, it was simply not what the people wanted.[2,3]

When Cadillac first landed on the shores of what he would call le détroit (The Straits) he could not have imagined how the land that stretched before him on three sides would be perfectly suited for the explosion of the automobile and the single-family-house-with-its-own-yard. Within the city limits of present day Detroit the maximum elevation change is less than 100 feet and that of the surrounding suburbs is quite similar.[4] Few cities in the US at the start of the 20th century had the advantage of convenient water transportation access and a seemingly endless expanse of flat land sprawling out in three directions. Detroit's first major roads, Grand River, Woodward, Gratiot, Jefferson, Michigan, and Fort Street spread out like the spokes of a wheel from the city's center. With this type of geographical layout the city had plenty of room to allow single-family homes to dominate, there was just too much buildable land easily accessible.[5] Before the demise of the Detroit area's mass transit systems, developers and land speculators in the outlying areas were instrumental in supporting these private companies to expand their lines. With the advent of the bus and car these same developers simply diverted their support to more and improved roadways.[6] This geographical landscape, once thought a blessing, ended up facilitating the growth of one of the Hydra's perpetual heads that finally led to the city's and region's extraordinary decline.

In the 1940's the Detroit Plan was formulated by city planners to facilitate the elimination of "blight" and the construction of a world-class freeway system. By the time construction started in the 1950's the administration of Mayor Albert E. Cobo concentrated heavily on freeway construction with little to no consideration for the urban renewal noted in the original plan. As a result when neighborhoods were plowed us under to make way for a new freeway the people and businesses in its path were basically ignored. This was politically viable as many of the areas in the path of this new construction were the poor, black-dominated slums near downtown and on the near east side. The new Chrysler Expressway running from downtown to Pontiac was placed right on top of Hastings Street just to the north east of Brush Park. Hastings Street was the core of the Black community in downtown and removing it eliminated its poor yet vibrant heart and soul. Even worse, due to the limited amount of affordable housing available to Blacks at the time, this action created significant stress on an already dismal situation.[7]

The new Chrysler Expressway lay on the east side of Brush Park essentially cutting this neighborhood off, along with the residents of Alfred Street, from the east side of the city. Along the south (river) side of Brush Park the Fisher Freeway (I-75) was built cutting these residents off from downtown. In addition to isolating the people left living in Brush Park and non-organically dividing up once functioning neighborhoods, the longer-term damage was that these roads allowed people to live further and further from the city center. Just like the original spoke-like arterials built in Detroit, these newly constructed freeways sprang forth in three directions emanating from the city's center. But unlike their predecessors these limited access roadways were not meant to facilitate commerce between those driving them and the areas in which they passed through. They were merely a conduit from here to there, a barren desert which one only used to travel from work to home. These freeways, combined with the large amount of buildable land, allowed easy perpetuation of the single-family-detached-home American dream. First those that could moved further out away from the crowded downtown. Then later racial and economic conflict pushed these people beyond the Detroit City limits. Once this exodus of the middle class started so did the tax base the City required to function. The second of the Hydra's heads had materialized.

It is difficult to exaggerate the level of racial hatred leading up to and after the riot of 1967 in Detroit. Even though Blacks in Detroit had a path out of the ghetto that those in other major metropolitan areas did not via relatively high paying jobs associated with the auto industry, the institutionalized prejudice of the White majority was still tremendously oppressive. This was most evident in the Black population that had not yet realized a path out of the poor living conditions they had experienced all their lives. Though in 1967 the population of Detroit was almost 40% black they made up less than 5% of the police force.[8] Police forces, like most government-run entities, are very slow to react and reflect the changing demographic of the people they are supposed to be serving. Elected officials usually respond to this changing demographic fairly quickly as they still need to get the votes of those living in the area at any given time. Matter of fact prior to the 1967 riot Detroit Mayor Jerome Cavanagh and his police chief Ray Girardin were considered some of the most progressive in the nation in their response to problems of the inner city. But they really did not run the day-to-day operations of the City, the life-long employees with un-fireable positions did.[9] For all the good, yet paternal, intensions of the White liberals at the time Blacks still had to contend with the underlying racial hatred that was generations in the making.

*'Oh sure, I guess Cavanagh tried to do something,' said a 23-year-old Negro, "but once a cop, always a cop. Girardin's a very nice wrinkled old man, but you can't change a Police Department in five years. It's still the career cops who run the department, and the career cop – like old 'Chew Tobacco Red' down in the 13ᵗʰ Precinct – hates niggers ... They come up to you on the street and say 'Hey, Boy!' Now there ain't nothin' on this driver's license that says 'boy.' They say 'Nigger, I'd like to kill you. ... You can swear out a complaint if a cop punches you, but what can you do if he calls you 'boy?'[10]*

As the 1960's came to a close this institutionalized abuse only motivated the Blacks that could to move further out from the inner city where they hoped it would be minimized. For the Whites in these outlining areas the influx of Blacks into their neighborhood highlighted their irrational fears and motivated them to move out of the City entirely.

As the 1970's dawned decisions by the federal courts would finally push the already diminishing White population in Detroit past the legal boundaries of the city completely. Originating in a suit brought by the NAACP against the Detroit Board of Education in 1971 and culminating in the landmark US Supreme Court case *Milliken v. Bradley, 418 U.S. 717 (1974)*, desegregation via forced busing of public school children was deemed legal only within existing school district boundaries. I myself was caught up in this upheaval. All I can recall of this time was the intense fear expressed by the adults around me that I would be forcibly bused from my idyllic home in the suburb of Trenton to a dilapidated, violence-ridden school in downtown Detroit. Whether or not this would have actually occurred had the Supreme Court's tally swung by one vote I know not, but the impression left upon me at that early age was indicative of that experienced by White children throughout the suburbs of Detroit. When the

Supreme Court reversed the District Court's plan to integrate Detroit public schools by pooling them with 53 suburban districts, it essentially set up school district boundaries as de facto barriers between Black and White populations. Whether the Court's opinion holding a narrower interpretation of the constitution was correct, whether the District Court's plan if implemented would have really made any difference in race relations in the area, or whether one agrees with Justice Marshall's dissent that "unless our children begin to learn together, there is little hope that our people will ever learn to live together,"[11] the point is now moot. For our story all that is important is that it did occur and thus facilitated the final mass exodus of the White population from Detroit. It also laid the foundation for the area's current demographics which leaves the City of Detroit with a Black population exceeding 80% and the vast majority of the surrounding suburbs with a White majority exceeding 90%.[12,13,14] The Hydra adds another head.

Meanwhile back on Alfred Street by the mid-1960's the Ransom Gillis House was abandoned by the Essas. Hemmed in on the southeast and northeast by the Fisher and Chrysler freeways and on the northwest by the expanding Medical Centers and Wayne State University, the Brush Park area avoided the renewal-wrecking ball of the 1950's and early 1960's intended to "improve" similar "blighted" areas.[15] Unfortunately its proximity to the original enclave (or ghetto) of Black Bottom meant that it saw a great exodus of middle-class Blacks during this period. It also suffered from the civil unrest and riot of 1967 eventually leaving the area disproportionally older, poorer, less educated, and crime-ridden. But there was still a seemingly unquenchable glimmer of hope for the area, and this time it originated from inside the neighborhood itself.

-------------------------------------------------------------------------------

In the summer of 1969 Edith Woodberry stood in an abandoned lot in the Brush Park neighborhood very near the Ransom Gillis House. The starkly barren lot was strewn with garbage and debris along with the remnants of a delivery truck and van both of which were missing all their windows. They had obviously been there for a while. The scene looked remarkably similar to what we in the first decade of the 21st century have come to expect from reporting in the Gaza Strip or Sadr City.[16] Edith was the president of a local non-profit organization named the Woodward East Project that was made up of people living in the Brush Park area. Though the population of the area had consistently dwindled as those Blacks that could, moved to better housing in outlining areas of Detroit, there still remained about 17,000 people there. Due to the out-migration of young middle-class families a disproportionate number of those left behind were senior citizens. The area had few public recreational facilities, especially those accessible to the predominately low-income population. "For this reason and because people do not like being cooped up in small, dilapidated rooms, there is a demand for numerous small parks where residents can relax, talk, and enjoy themselves," stated one of the organization's first publications.[17] But Woodward East's primary objective was to provide decent housing for the people left in the area. Many of the large and once grand houses in the area were occupied by renters and in very poor condition. The abandoned, gutted car and truck bodies scattered around the vacant lots  where burned out houses had been torn down were frequently used by the local homeless for sleeping. Other homeless would sleep on the porches of abandoned houses in the summer and break into them in the winter, sometimes setting them on fire in an effort to keep warm.[18]

Woodward East Project was formed in 1967 with the help of the Downtown Churches Action Mission (all churches together in our neighborhood) that also helped create a number of other community action groups at the time. Some of the other groups formed at the time to address the problems in the area were; Brush Park Citizens Association, St. Patrick's

Community Council, Brush Park Property Owners, Brush Park Tenants' Council Improvement Association, Women's Improvement Council, and Brewster Tenant Council.[19,20,21] Of all of these groups though, Woodward East rose to become the most active primarily due to the tenacity and perseverance of its originator and leader Edith Woodberry.[22] Edith, a mother of 12 and a resident of the area, was the driving force behind Woodward East from the start. Under Edith's leadership her group pursued its main emphasis of providing decent housing for many of their low income and homeless neighbors. For all its energy and good intentions Woodward East, as an organization for change, was doomed from the outset by its very nature. Although officially formed as a non-profit corporation, Woodward East was at its base a volunteer group. Its members were by nature of where they lived, low-income so their primary mode of support of the organization was simple manual labor. The organization itself had little to no funding sources (the dues were $1 to join) and thus was totally dependent on donations and outside grants. They had no taxing authority as a government would, though they quickly tried to tackle problems that the City, County, or State governments had persistently neglected and ignored for years. They had no products to sell like a for-profit company thus they had no funds to sustain their members as they spent hundreds of unpaid hours trying to improve their neighborhood. Woodward East held meetings at least once a week, initiated with a prayer usually led by Bishop Rosa Jones, which were strictly voluntary. As the organization grew and they took on more and more projects these meetings sometimes expanded to 5 different ones on separate issues in one day. They eventually took on the responsibilities of a small government or business, yet they had not the funds to retain the people necessary for such an organization or to develop the procedures and structure needed to successfully carry out the projects that they tackled. Inevitably, as is common in ad hoc organizations of this type, they soon ran up against the fact that their membership could only spend a limited amount of time on these efforts. They all had jobs to do to make a living; they quickly suffered from a perceived lack of involvement of their members. Though they had vibrant energy towards their own self-determination, there was simply not a basis for the monetary or personnel resources to facilitate such an effort. Initially this did not deter them or quash Edith's resolve to her community, they were heart-set on improving the miserable living conditions their neighbors had to contend with. Thus they pushed forward with their efforts despite the deficiencies in their organization. If they did not no one else would. One of the first problem properties they addressed was on the opposite side of the street and six houses down from the Ransom Gillis House, an apartment complex at 268 Alfred Street.[23,24,25]

The building at 268 Alfred Street (96 Alfred prior to street renumbering in the 1920's) was originally a grand Victorian structure like all the rest on the street at the dawning of the 19th century. When the Blue Bloods fled and the houses on the street were converted to rooming by the 1920's the then owners of the structure at 268 Alfred took this process one step further. They extended the structure all the way to the alley between Alfred and Adelaide, more than tripling its size. It became more of a full-fledged apartment building instead of a simple rooming house. Maybe this was the reason that while many of the old mansions in Brush Park were abandoned by the 1960's this structure still had paying tenants, albeit the shelter that these tenants were paying for was woefully deficient. The problems in this building and the landlord's resistance or inability to correct them were one of the Woodward East's first missions.[26]

Quickly becoming the "place to go" if you had problems in the community, Woodward East soon started fielding complaints about the conditions in which the residents of 268 Alfred were having to contend with. In the spring of 1969 it was "brought to the meeting (Woodward East Project meeting) a statement concerning a lawsuit brought against the owner of the building at 268 Alfred where rats and roaches are about to take over and there is no hot water or heat."[27] In March of that year, after this lawsuit was filed, a Wayne County Circuit Court judge took the building away from the owners and placed it in receivership to be handled by Woodward East. In the following few months Woodward East made progress improving the condition of the building but this was thwarted by a fire that gutted the building that summer. After this the judge returned the building to the original owners in preparation for them to either rehabilitate it with their insurance settlement, sell it, or tear it down.[28] Woodward East soon purchased the building and within the next year many of the other neglected structures, some inhabited, some abandoned, in the area. They then attempted to maintain and improve them the best they could with their limited funds and predominantly volunteer labor. These buildings, perhaps too many considering the structure and resources of their organization, included, 224 Erskine, 261 Alfred, 54 Alfred, 231 Winder, 245 Edmund Place, 229 Edmund Place, 52 Alfred, 268 Alfred, 418 Watson, 287 Alfred, and 107 Erskine.[29] But early on in their planning, before they were momentarily distracted by pressing matters at 268 Alfred, Woodward East had their sights on Henry T. Brush's then abandoned structure at the corner John R. and Alfred.[30]

In the February 13th, 1969 meeting of the Woodward East Project Edith Woodberry told those assembled that the next building they were going to purchase was 205 Alfred Street. She also noted that this property had a store in front. Obviously the storefront that the Essa's had added decades earlier was still intact and presumably functional though the overall building was abandoned.[31] As was common with actions in the early days of Woodward East things moved quickly. Perhaps they moved too quickly but then again it had been so long since anything had happened to improve the neighborhood maybe it was deemed that the people had to see some type of progress lest they lose hope. At any rate, by March 3$^{rd}$ of that year the law firm working with Woodward East had told them that the property at 205 Alfred was now theirs. This assertion in early 1969 is somewhat in contradiction to the deed associated with the property as that notes that the Essa's did not sell the property to Woodward East until January 9, 1973. Perhaps Woodward East seeing an abandoned building in their neighborhood took it upon themselves to correct the situation. Having been forgotten by the Essa's maybe the legal assistance the organization was receiving (likely pro bono) did not uncover the former owners claim on the property. Most likely a few years later, once the Essa's who had already moved to the suburbs became aware of what Woodward East was doing, they asked for payment for the property.[32,33]

In typical fashion within 10 days Edith had mobilized her volunteer forces and set them upon 205 Alfred. Soon there was a cleanup crew working to pick up garbage that had accumulated around the house and the City had been contacted to send a truck to haul it away. Already 13 toilets had been donated for installation at 205 Alfred to replace the interior fixtures that had suffered from years of neglect and abandonment.[34] Within a week or two a volunteer crew was dispatched to the building under the direction of Clarence Welcome to clear out the debris that had accumulated inside. After being a rooming house for 40 years and then being left to the ravages of the local homeless population, there was not much of the interior that could be salvaged. After some work to this end, Mr. Welcome attended the March 27$^{th}$ meeting of Woodward East to facilitate some more assistance. At that meeting,

*He wanted to know if he could get permission to seek expert help on plumbing, electricity, etc. It was motioned by Mr.*

*Dent that he should be given permission to seek the help he needs. It was seconded and carried.*[35]

This exchange speaks much louder than it at first may seem. With close observation it cuts to the core problems that faced the Woodward East Project at this time. Problems of which they were probably still not aware, but ones that would eventually lead to the failure of their noble efforts. First, since a significant amount of the labor conducted by this organization was volunteer it was by its very nature done by people lacking specific experience of the task at hand. Thus when Mr. Welcome and his crew of well-meaning people embarked on the rehabilitation of the Ransom Gillis House, initially their efforts were productive as they simply entailed the manual labor of cleaning up the worthless material in the house and on the surrounding property. Quickly though they ran into items which they rightfully knew that they did not have the capability of doing properly and thus asked for "permission" to find someone who had these skills. Unfortunately, once they needed the work of skilled trades like plumbers and electricians they knew that this would come at a cost. Thus they had to go back before the whole organization to get approval and eventually funds. The cost of items like this was one issue due to the tenuous funding Woodward East was always under, but more important logistically was the need to constantly go before the whole organization to move these issues forward. Traditionally in a construction project like this there would be a project manager who was given a specific budget for the job. The amount of this budget determined how much he could do prior to doing anything at all. This seemed not to be the case as Woodward East approached the rehabilitation of the Ransom Gillis House. The organization as a whole seemed to be taking on the position of project manager and the funds that could be spent on this project were not specified in advance. Thus the scope of what actually could be done was not really defined. This approach was understandable at the time due to the limited experience Woodward East had in conducting projects of this magnitude and the fact that they had a burning desire to "do something." Unfortunately this approach was fraught with danger. The situation became even more dangerous if not disastrous the deeper they moved into projects in which they had not the organizational structure to control. Later on they did try to assemble such a rudimentary structure but it ended up being too little and too late for the structures in Brush Park. But at the close of the 1960's though they were experiencing symptoms of these ailments, they had not yet succumbed to the disease and plodded onward with plans to build a new vision of the area in which they wanted to or had no choice but to live. Of course the City of Detroit and other outside entities that worked with Woodward East during this time were equally blind to the inherent structural flaws in their organization and did little to rectify the situation before it got too far along. This did not deter a number of outside organizations from becoming involved with Woodward East's efforts. One wonders though if these mostly White, middle-class outside organizations were doing so out of an honest desire to help in the renewal of the area or out of paternal guilt for being a contributing factor to the area's decline in the first place. It was also questionable if this outside help had the commitment to stick with this effort for the tediously long duration it would obviously entail. One of the first groups to temporarily help Woodward East was the faculty and students of the University of Detroit's Architecture department in August of 1969. But their involvement was short-lived involving only some plans for frontage on Woodward Avenue.[36,37] Woodward East continued in this mode doing what they could for their community through the first few years of the 1970's. In 1975 though things started to heat up.

On July 15th, 1975 a representative of Lawrence Institute of Technology's School of Architecture attended a Detroit

Common Council meeting in the County Building downtown. There Mrs. Groehn from Lawrence Tech presented some sketches recently done by students in the Architectural History III class at the university in support of a project to renew a 9-1/2 acre area in Brush Park. On the far southwest edge of this plot sat what remained of the Ransom Gillis House. Mrs. Groehn left the meeting with a commendation from the council thanking "the School of Architecture of Lawrence Institute of Technology, it's students and faculty, for their interest and involvement in the concerns and hopes for the city."[38]

The area to be redeveloped was entitled the Woodward East Renaissance and was bordered by John R to the southwest, Brush Street to the northeast, Alfred Street to the southeast, and the alley behind the houses on Watson Street to the northwest. A preliminary sketch of the proposed renovation produced by William Kessler and Associates showed a perspective view of the site fronting Alfred Street. In the far left-hand corner was a rough, historically inaccurate, depiction of the Ransom Gillis House. The lot next door, originally 69 Alfred, was shown as vacant occupied only by a few newly planted trees. Obviously the structure that had actually housed the Gillis family for the greater part of their time on the street was already gone. The plan was for 18 of the remaining Victorian structures to be converted to apartments. The balance of the land on the site, much of which was already vacant or contained structures too far gone to save, would be cleared and in its place 104 housing units constructed along with ample open, communal spaces. The layout with its trellised walkways, brick paved common spaces, and playgrounds was truly idyllic, a walkers paradise. Matter of fact, the sketch showed pedestrians strolling along its tree lined sidewalks and walkways, numerous people milling around the brick paved plazas, and children on the playground, but ironically in the heart of the Motor City, less than 10 automobiles were shown. Wishful thinking considering that hundreds of people, many of them middle-class, would be living in the area.[39]

The vehicle behind the Woodward East Renaissance was none other than the Woodward East Project, Inc. The scope of this project was far beyond anything Edith and the other members of Woodward East had ever attempted. It would require orders of magnitude more logistical control. But this was the light at the end of the tunnel, it looked as if all their hard work and struggles over the last 7 years were actually going to make a change in their neighborhood. They were hopeful. By 1975 Edith and her organization had solicited funding from various State, Federal, and Local sources including the National Endowment for the Arts and the National Trust for Historic Preservation. Later that year twenty local and regional architects, some quite prominent, gathered in a room with numerous drawings scattered on a number of large drafting tables. They had gathered there, donating three days of their time, in an effort to generate the required documents needed to obtain further financing for the project. Along with the design professionals present, all of whom were White, there were two Black people representing the local community, Edith Woodberry, already in her late 40's, and Mike Johnson who functioned as the project manager for Woodward East.[40,41]

For the next few years plans were drawn up and work was started on the project under the direction of the Woodward East Project, Inc. Mike Johnson served as the Project Manager and Edith continued her role as community and political activist for the area as well as the President of Woodward East. In 1976, being the Bicentennial year, a lot of money flowed into the area for this restoration effort. But Woodward East still was plagued with their organizational challenges. They also wanted to direct as much of the restoration work as possible to local people and firms. Most of the buildings needed much more than the local work force could accommodate.  As progress was not apparent or as much as expected, more money was simply thrown at the project without the proper controls in place to manage and monitor it.  In the end a lot of money was wasted and only some simple framing was completed before the city shut down the project.  Although there were allegations of money being stolen, the real problem was the overall management, or lack thereof.[42]

It was probably during this time that the store in front of the Ransom Gillis House was torn down.  Sometime prior to 1977 everything associated with this storefront except two of the exterior walls had disappeared.[43]  It is not known if this was the result of work associated with the Woodward East Renaissance, vandalism, or a combination of both.  Other than the removal of the storefront the only other significant work on the house during this period seems to be the gutting of the remnants of the interior by Mr. Welcome and his volunteer crew back in 1969.

Undeterred by the lack of progress on the Woodward East Renaissance project, Edith and Michael remained committed to their neighborhood though naïve about the overwhelming obstacles in their path.  In February of 1978 both attended a three day conference in Baltimore entitled, "Thinking Small: Transportation's Role in Neighborhood Revitalization" sponsored by the US Department of Transportation.  On the morning of the second day of this conference Edith gave a presentation entitled "Woodward East."  Interestingly immediately following there was a presentation given by Harriet Sherburne on the "Pike Place Market Renewal," a location this author has visited many times during my 23 years living in the Seattle area.  During a discussion on the effectiveness of using small-scale transportation alternatives like Dial-A-Rides or vanpools Edith commented, "We have come up with an idea in our own area. We have about five young people in the neighborhood who make it a point of driving people from our community any place they want to go. All anyone has to do is call up and say, 'Hey, I need a ride.' It can be completely out to suburbia or wherever." A nice idea but obviously not reliable in the long run. Ideas like this, well intentioned but unfeasible without rudimentary logistics, controls, and administration, eventually doomed her company's efforts at renewal.[44]

In the Fall of 1985 just as winter was preparing to make its annual onslaught on the Detroit area, Michigan Consolidated Gas Company (MichCon) shut off the flow of natural gas to the boiler at 445 Fisher Freeway that supplied heat and hot water to the 18 units there. This was one of the last properties in the area managed by Edith Woodberry now via the Woodward East Management and Rental Company. MichCon along with a number of other creditors forced Edith and her company into involuntary Chapter 7 bankruptcy on December 4th of that year.[45] Two years earlier, on October 1st of 1983 the Woodward East Project, which had originally initiated the grand plans for the Woodward East Renaissance had gone through automatic dissolution.[46] A few years prior the Woodward East Project had already lost the property on which the Ransom Gillis House stood to the State of Michigan for back taxes. By the time Edith's first company dissolved, the City of Detroit had acquired the land and house at the corner of Alfred and John R from the State. Thus ended before it had really even started, the first effort to save the structure that Henry T. Brush had designed some 100 years earlier.[47,48] Though the efforts by the Woodward East Project and its facilitators failed, dreams of repairing the mansions in the Brush Park area were not abandoned.

------------------------------------------------------------------------

As the 1980's dawned, middle and upper class homeowners were starting to move back into the heart of major cities in the US. In Philadelphia, San Francisco, and New York this influx was substantial along with the displacement of the poorer, mainly minority, occupants originally there. In Detroit at this time there was only a trickle. Those few that did come in did so on their own with little to no government or other outside help. One article written in 1984 called them "Urban Pioneers." Brush Park along with a few other areas in the city with historic but forgotten homes saw individualized attempts at this private, small-scale renewal throughout the 1980's. This was usually attempted by young, idealistic professionals who understood the history they were trying to save but underestimated the monumental effort needed to save it.[49] These sporadic efforts where fraught with numerous obstacles and those who attempted it sometimes felt as they were going it alone, much like a homesteader on the Kansas prairie in the 1800's. First to contend with was the decades-long issue of race that facilitated the flight of middle-income Whites to the suburbs in the first place. Mark Mardirosian and his wife bought a house in Detroit's Woodbridge neighborhood just north of Brush Park, he lamented in 1984 on why others have not followed them there, "It's a racial issue...when it boils down to it, suburban people don't move in because it's black and it's Detroit. People are incredibly determined to live in Birmingham. It's like Birmingham or nothing, whatever the price."[50] Then there was the issue of crime. Though they had an alarm system for their house, Mardirosian noted, "We're extremely vulnerable here ... I hate to even think of how many things we've lost out of our garage."[51] Another pioneer who rehabilitated a house in Brush park starting in the early 1980's commented jokingly to a reporter as he left the house after an interview, "Oh, great. Your car is still here."[52] Lastly, there was the battle against the background mentality of the metropolitan area. Mike Kirk an architect out of University of Michigan who worked directly with Edith Woodberry and Michael Johnson in their attempts to accomplish the Woodward East Renaissance less than a decade earlier lamented, "We're the auto town. We're chrome and glass and we throw everything away every year. That has been the big problem."[53]

But the biggest problems these pioneers faced were ones systemic to Detroit and in many cases insurmountable, City bureaucracy and mortgage financing. The bureaucracy at the time was dominated by the City's Community and Economic Development Department (C&EDD). Most of these pioneers could not understand why the city would be keeping people from trying to fix these once great structures before they crumbled to the ground. Some people trying to rehab properties in Brush Park thought that they were being ignored by the City because the land was being held for something else. There were rumors of a yearlong floral exhibition or a world's fair planned for the site.[54] On the shadier side there were rumors that the redevelopment of Brush Park was blocked up due to a brothel that was run out of a house on Watson Street. It was frequented by prominent politicians in the city and the innkeeper did not want all the attention the newfound residents would bring.[55] The City due to the experiences in Brush Park in the 1970's could have also been hesitant to do anything. As with many government entities doing nothing means that you cannot be accused of doing anything wrong. Finally there was the issue of financing. With the City showing little interest in saving these structures, private mortgages were hard to come by. Banks did not want to lend the money to even bring the buildings into a habitable condition as if the homeowner did not succeed the bank would be left with a property that was essentially worthless. The value was not in the property itself, as it is in most real estate deals, it was in the potential value of the property once the rehabilitation had gotten to a certain state. Before the structure was brought up to that minimal state, the bank's investment was not supported by any real capital. Bankers usually assign very little value to hope. Alas, the few houses that were rehabilitated during this time were basically financed by the homeowners themselves.[56]

At this time the Ransom Gillis House was not yet unrecoverable. The roof was still primarily intact albeit many of the slate shingles were gone and the wooden slats they were originally attached to exposed to the elements. The dormer in the front of the house was leaning ever so slightly in towards the building suggesting the impending structural failure of the roof trusses leading to the collapse of the roof and associated enhanced exposure of the interior to the elements. Any remnants of the original wrought iron cresting on the roof were gone. Remarkably the cone roof atop the signature turret on the front corner of the house was completely intact less the ornamental iron Tower Finial that was lost some time after 1977.[57] The turret itself had just recently started to visibly pull away from the rest of the structure even though its supporting column had been absent for decades now. Two walls remained of the storefront attached to the corner of the house by John Essa and his family. On one of these remaining non-brick walls was a half torn sign promoting the candidacy of Delores Bennett.[58] The stop sign out in front marking the corner of John R and Alfred Street was tipped gently about 10 degrees off vertical and faced in the wrong direction.[59] The structure's main public exposure during this time was a prominent 4-second cameo during the opening credits of the 1984 release of Beverly Hills Cop.[60] Into this fray jumped one Douglas Kuykendall.

On November 13, 1985 Douglas Kuykendall and his sister purchased what was left of the Ransom Gillis House for $1,000 from the City of Detroit. Prior to this, in September of that same year they entered in to a Development Agreement with the City concerning the property.[61] Douglas, a lifetime resident of the East Side of Detroit whose parents moved there from the South around WWII, is who we have to thank for saving the iconic turret on the corner of the structure. The removal of the ornate turret support post and base by the Essas to facilitate the storefront transferred this elements load to the roof of the store. Once the store ebbed away after the Essas left, the turret was left unsupported. By the time Douglas acquired the property the storefront had been reduced to just two walls, leaving the turret clinging to the rest of the structure predominantly via the shear force on the ancient brick and mortar. Terrified that the turret would very soon come tumbling to the ground, one of Douglas' first tasks was to support it from underneath like the original ornate masonry base and post designed by Henry T. Brush had done. Unfortunately Douglas did not have the resources Henry had in the 1870's, so he improvised and supported it with an iron pipe. This pipe alone remained as the only defense provided to the turret from the unrelenting onslaught of gravity for the next two decades. Without this effort the turret would have surely been lost and I would have never paused and pondered the history of this structure on that sunny summer day in 2004.[62]

Douglas had bought the structure as he was enamored by its "grand architecture."[63] His friends thought he was crazy to undertake this project on his own, yet a few of them ended up helping him in this effort. The restaurant behind the house, built on the ground where the original stable was located, the stable that served as the original home for Pewbic Pottery, was vacant. It was included with his purchase of the house and property so Douglas decided to make use of it as a workshop to support his construction effort. First though he had to fix its leaking roof and more importantly secure the building so that his tools would not "walk off" overnight. As with the "Urban Pioneers" theft was a frustrating problem. As Douglas lamented about the time, "when we went home at night they came in and appropriated materials ... we come back again the next day and start over again."[64] Initially the house was not habitable. The roof was far worse than a casual view from the street would imply, nature had full access to the house's interior. The once ornate interior details were gone by this time, "no woodwork and cornices or anything like that, no that had all melted away from the weather and vandalism."[65] The first thing, after supporting the turret, was to fix the roof to keep the weather out. The proper way to approach this task was first to surround the structure with metal scaffolding. Access to a small crane would surely be needed to repair the failing trusses on the roof. Scaffolding may also have been needed inside what was left of the structure. Douglas had the resources for none of this. All he had the capital and equipment to construct was some rather precarious wooden scaffolding made of 2x4's and 2x6's along the front portion of the house. An admirable effort, but far short of what was needed.[66,67] There would be accusations years later that Douglas did not live up to some of the requirements to rehab the structure, but one would think that the former owner, the City of Detroit, would have had the where-with-all to inform the person purchasing this property of the magnitude of the task he was undertaking.[68]

As with the others who attempted to rehab the once stately structures in Brush Park, financing was a problem. One of the factors motivating Douglas to purchase the property were loans and other financial assistance promised by the City. He thought that the City would at least facilitate with entities either public or private so that he could get the capital he sorely needed to have any chance of saving the structure. The funds never materialized.[69] With the structure in imminent danger of collapse and Douglas trying to prevent it with the meager resources he could acquire, City government seemed more of a hindrance than anything else. "They would cruise around and anytime you would begin to do anything they would magically show up and say 'oh you can't do that, you got a permit for this?'"[70] The records of the Detroit Historic District Commission do show that the construction of "a 4 to 5 foot high fence around the property" was applied for and approved in 1986. These records also show that Douglas applied to the commission "to change property from single family dwelling to apartments, and to repair slate roof" in 1987.[71] This last request is interesting and lends some anecdotal credence to the view that the City's implementation of their laws and ordinances was somewhat haphazard and confusing. Douglas had to apply in 1987 to get approval to change the building to an apartment while in fact it had been being used for that very purpose since the Fikes left some time before 1920. The City's official records were over 67 years out of date! Eventually the City became hostile to his efforts, it seemed they just wanted the property back. Douglas was running into problems similar to those faced by others attempting to save some of Detroit's old structures in the 1980's. It seemed "the city's administration may be more interested in demolition, commercial development and land banking than residential restoration."[72] It makes you wonder why the City sold these buildings to these individuals in the first place. After about 5 years, investing a lot of sweat equity and frustration, Douglas abandoned his effort. Eventually in June of 2001 the City of Detroit acquired the property back via eminent domain paying Douglas and his sister $329,560.[73]

As a final insult there appeared an article in the Detroit News on 9/26/2005 entitled *How Not to Rebuild Detroit*. A portion of this article dealt specifically with the Ransom Gillis House, reporter David Josar wrote:

> *Instead of using nuisance abatement laws and other legal tools to fight blight, the city has stood by as speculators snatched up properties, kept the buildings vacant and then done so little maintenance the house are uninhabitable. Douglas Kuykendall and Ernestine Rooks in 1985 bought the Gillis Mansion at 205 Alfred from the city for $1,500, according to Wayne County court records. A development agreement required them to make repairs and occupy the property within a year, according to court records. That never happened. Instead, in 2004, after the mansion had lost*

*its roof and its chimneys had crumbled, Detroit agreed to pay Kuykendall and Rooks $329,659 for the home to settle a lawsuit filed by the city seeking to seize and condemn the property. Watkins said the city should not be blamed for the condition of the Gillis Mansion because it got title only recently. Still the development agreement allowed the city to take possession of the Gillis Mansion after Kuykendall and Rooks failed to rehab the property as they had promised. "That's disgusting," said Sanderson, who bought his home on Erskine at the same time Kuykendall and Rooks purchased theirs. "This could have been stopped," said Sanderson, flipping through fading color photographs of the mansions that were still standing when he began rehabbing his home in the 1980s. "The city decided it didn't want to do that." The loss of properties by what has come to be known as "demolition by neglect" is heartbreaking, said Patricia Linklater, chairman of the Detroit Historic District Commission. If officials had made sure the people acquiring city-owned buildings kept their promises or had them 'mothballed' properly so they could be restored once development was on an upswing, Detroit would have one of the greatest downtown historic districts in the nation, she said. 'There is no measuring what has been lost,' Linklater said. 'What has happened here is a shame, it's an embarrassment,'[74]*

Douglas was never contacted in reference to this article in the Detroit News, maybe if he had been the public would have understood the problem was a bit more complicated with its roots planted far earlier than the 1980's.[75] The City had acquired the property yet again at the dawn of the 21st century as they had another renewal project in mind.

---

Throughout the 1990's plans continued to surface from various community groups, organizations, and the City to redevelop and/or restore what remained of the Brush Park area. Throughout this time there was controversy on what this rebirth should look like. Many of the existing, lower-income residents worried that development would force them out of the only homes they could afford. But probably more decisive was the simple logistics of living in an area of high crime and incessant drug dealing, with not even a local grocery store where you could buy a gallon of milk. Not an inviting environment for young middle-income families of which the area sorely needed for its health. Even the very few "Urban Pioneers" who were able to restore a small number of the ancient structures began to lose hope that a true restoration of the Victorian grandeur of the area would ever be possible.[76] Then Crosswinds Communities entered the picture. By 1999 Crosswinds Communities, a company originated in the Detroit area, started building housing in the Brush Park area.[77] By 2003 they had developed a conceptual plan to redevelop the southern-most section of Brush Park between Woodward and Brush Street and from I-75 to Alfred Street. The plan included all the remaining Victorian structures, including the Ransom Gillis House, on the north side of Alfred Street.[78] At this time the Ransom Gillis house was in the condition we were first introduced to it at the beginning of this book. There was significant fire damage. The roof had caved in upon itself and the thick red brick walls now stood open to the sky above. Small sections of the slate tile roof were still barely visible from the street along with one small remnant of the iron cresting, hinting to the new visitor the grandeur of its past. Surprisingly most of the inlay tile work scattered strategically around the front of the structure was still intact, especially that on the turret. The turret, that magnificent detail that separated this structure from those around it, was still there, though leaning even more precariously, still there for passerby's to ponder, saved by the iron post put there by Douglas Kuykendall almost 20 years prior. In the summer months most of this detail

107

was obscured by lush green undergrowth of varying heights around the base of the structure. Some of these bushes had actually migrated into the structure itself showing themselves on what remained of the roof and through the open windows of the turret. In the winter months, this foliage lost its greenery and when there was a light dusting of snow the structure took on its most desolate and foreboding appearance.[79]

About a year after I originally happened upon the structure, I was contacted by Randy Wilcox. Randy had been taking an interest and pictures of many of the ruins in Detroit since about 2000. By the time we communicated in September of 2005 he had already been inside the Ransom Gillis House three times. Whereas elsewhere people spelunk into naturally occurring underground caves, many in Detroit had taken up the hobby of urban spelunking, exploring the once grand ruins that littered many areas of the city. This was far more dangerous than cave spelunking, as one never knew if the failure of a roof truss, floor joist, or other load-bearing component of the structure was imminent. But Randy was of the opinion, like many in the area who partook in this dangerous and mostly illegal activity, "All I can say is I am very cautious and try not to get smooshed...My lust for capturing what's left of the interiors is what motivates my reckless behavior."[80] A few days after our first contact, and without my prodding I might add, I received a bundle of pictures from the inside of the house. Taken on September 9th, 2005 these images encompassed the final and perhaps the only detailed visual record of the inside of the Ransom Gillis House. Many have lived there over its lifetime but only this courageous spelunker had documented it.

Randy entered the structure via one for the remaining basement windows that had not been bricked over. Approaching his effort like an archeologist exploring some ancient Egyptian tomb, he first noted that, "It is certainly not the safest structure to be in, but it has been so destroyed on the interior that there simply isn't much left to collapse on you when you're inside."[81] Most of the floors in the structure were gone, some joists remained precariously in place but they were not numerous enough to block the view of the crisp blue autumn sky above. The untrained, impatient observer would have assumed that nothing of worth remained, but this was not the case. Looking closely, carefully, with full knowledge of the history of those who had lived there, the secrets of the house began to emerge. Looking to the southwest up towards the only remaining intact chimney in the structure the hearth of a fireplace on the second floor could be seen. Though one could not be sure due to the distance, it looked like the mantle above this fireplace remained, almost completely intact made of a white marble slab. One could imagine this might have been the location of Alanson Fox's "famous library" where Mary Chase negotiated her initial rental of the carriage house which she then turned into the first home of Pewabic Pottery.

More impressive, if one had enough imagination, was the interior view of the iconic turret in the corner of the structure. Though this part of the structure was unapproachable from the only stable horizontal surface in the building, the basement floor, one could just make out the turret's interior protrusion from this location. The collapsed floor joists and roof trusses huddled in this corner seemed to provide a stairway to the turret but Randy knew far better, he was pressing his luck just being where he was. From this vantage point though one could get a feeling what the view from inside this turret would have been like. It was not that large, less than six feet in diameter, it was most probably used as a sitting area.[82] Perhaps there was a window bench around its circumference where the children of the Fox's and later the Fikes' would sit and read. Surrounded by its original five tall windows sitting there one would have gotten the best light in the house, especially prior to the advent of electricity. If there was a bench it was most certainly covered with velvet cushions, maroon in color I would suppose. The five windows that surrounded the turret were probably covered by soft cream-colored lace valances, which allowed the maximum amount of natural light transmittance. In the summer months the bottom half of these windows would be raised to allow a soft breeze to enter. Sitting there, book in hand, one would have had a territorial view of the goings on at the corner of Alfred and John R. Even after the structure had been converted to a rooming house I am sure that the turret was still a coveted location, especially by the young. Sure the velvet cushions and lace valances were most certainly gone but the view was still grand, they probably viewed it as their own little tree fort.

Throughout what remained of the structure the original lath of the lath and plaster walls was present in many locations. Only a very few, sheltered areas retained any plaster, mostly it was just the lath, affixed directly to the load bearing brick walls. In the basement of the building this symmetrical, mathematically spaced brickwork gave way to a foundation of irregular but meticulously placed stone. Spattered within the structure there was also evidence of the remodeling that had occurred through the years. Here and there modern drywall complete with untaped screws or nails could be found. Someone, perhaps Douglas or even Woodward East had tried to cover the exposed studs, but they did not get too far. Ungrounded two prong outlets and the remnants of ancient knob and tube wiring remained, probably untouched since it was installed in the early 1900's.[83]

Upon Randy's further investigation he came upon one of the last remnants of the once ornate detailing inside the house. On the front wall was a section that was probably a sitting room for guests, just off what would have been the main hallway from the entrance to the building. In the open cavern that once contained this room, in one of the upper corners there remained two tattered examples of ornate plasterwork that once encircled its perimeter like crown molding.

The two remaining pieces were decorated with a leaf-like pattern looking like something you would find on the top of a roman Corinthian column. On the basement floor laid a small piece of this ornamental plasterwork that had left its original location far above some time earlier. Randy picked it up carefully, respectfully, as if it were the jawbone of some long extinct Velocoraptor. Randy later noted, "I recovered a chunk of plaster detail from the debris on the east side of the house near where the plaster remains up on the second story ceiling. It was like powdered chalk and extremely fragile, but still maintains a surprising amount of detail. The plaster had been slowly melting in the moisture over the years, but this chunk still has some relief left to it. I set the exterior with thick clear pottery glaze to save the piece."[84] Hence this adventurous urban spelunker probably saved the only remaining example of the once glorious interior details created by Henry T. Brush over 100 years earlier. This rescue was especially important seeing what was next in store for the structure.

The administration of then Mayor Kwame Kilpatrick wanted to demolish all four remaining Victorian structures on the north side of Alfred Street prior to the 2006 Superbowl just three blocks away at Ford Field. Luckily the City's Brush Park project manager was able to convince them that stabilizing the structure so that it had potential for renovation in the name of historic preservation would be money well spent in the long run.[85] So after purchasing the property, the City of Detroit invested about $350,000 to "mothball" the building. The object was not to return the structure to its original condition of 1879, but to salvage and stabilize what remained to buy some time, 5 to 10 years, in hopes to find a developer willing to do a detailed restoration.[86] Modern tube frame scaffolding was put up on the front and side of the building. There was also scaffolding placed under the turret along with temporary wood reinforcements of this part of the structure. This allowed safe access to the top of the building. A small crane was also used to remove what remained of the roof including some of the iron detailing. Unfortunately none of these iron remnants were saved, presumably they ended up in an arc metal recycling furnace somewhere in the area. Typical modern wood framing was then assembled in the cleared out interior of the building to facilitate the installation of a new asphalt shingled roof. Prior to the installation of the new roof trusses, the top parts of the exterior brick walls around a significant part of the circumference of the structure had to be rebuilt. Sections of the existing brick masonry that were unsound and crumbling were removed and replaced with new.[87,88] While this work was being conducted Peter Essa, the nephew of John and Amina Essa the owners of the house from the 1940's to 1970's stopped by. Peter routinely stopped by the house on his periodic trips to the VA Hospital nearby Brush Park. Peter a WWII veteran who spent a great deal of his childhood around his Uncle's store in front of the Ransom Gillis House and use to shoot rats in the basement with his cousins, liked to stop by and check on the structure. This time he was able to catch the attention of one of the contractors to whom he told his story. The worker sifted through the debris on the ground and came up with one of the original bricks that had fallen off the structure years ago. He presented it to Peter. Peter accepted it as one would a long lost family treasure.[89]

When the "mothballing" or "stabilization" was complete in March of 2006 the structure at the corner of John R and Alfred Street, where it had stood for over 120 years, seemed a shadow of its former self. The low maintenance and longevity of a modern asphalt shingled roof had supplanted the original slate tile and mansard's esthetically pleasing detail. Even the turret seemed somewhat tainted as the cone-shaped slate covering with its ornamental iron Tower Finial was replaced with a simple hexigonigal asphalt roof. The tall arched windows that once graced the circumference of the turret, their wooden frames neglected and exposed to the elements for far too long, could not be saved. They were replaced by a 2x4 framing covered with simple plywood. Amazingly when the temporary wood supports under the turret were removed when the construction was complete; a metal pole again provided the only underlying support of that part of the structure. It is not known if this was the support originally placed there by Douglas Kuykendall.[90] With the $329,560 paid to Douglas and his sister and $350,000 invested in the "mothballing," the City of Detroit had close to $700,000 invested in the structure. They estimated it would take another million to return it to any semblance of its original Victorian grandeur.[91] Unfortunately, a couple of years after this work was completed by the City, Crosswinds did not look like they would be in a position to carry through with the final restoration of the houses on Alfred Street as originally planned. Luckily the City of Detroit still held the title to the property.[92] A romantic might lament that the structure would have been better left as it was, as its prior state gave the observer an emotional hint of all it had been through. Now it just looked like an overdone track house in the suburbs. Alas no action at all would have been disastrous, as with a few more unprotected years all traces of the house's existence would have surely disappeared.

After this last temporary flurry of activity was completed in early 2006 the Ransom Gillis House was left alone. It again stood as it had for years dominating the corner of John R and Alfred Street remaining there though its neighbors were long gone. Further down Alfred towards Woodward there remained two houses in which the owners had actually managed to restore starting in the 1980's. The current occupiers of these again grand residences had for years hoped that others would follow them and return the neighborhood to its original Victorian grandeur. Now they had all but lost hope. Their plight reminded one of Charlton Heston hold up alone in his glorious penthouse apartment surrounded by memories of the world that once was in the 1970's classic Omega Man.[93]

# The Hydra

*"Detroit, the place where capitalism failed"*

*--Frank Rashid[1]*

On January 1st, 1901 the mayor of Detroit, William C. Maybury, placed some notes written by a selected few of the elite of the City of Detroit into a copper box. This box was then soldered shut not to be opened for 100 years. One hundred years later the then current mayor of Detroit, Dennis Archer, broke said seal and peered inside.[2] Inside this box was a letter written to the future people of Detroit by one of the prominent architects at the dawning of the 20th century, John M. Donaldson. As you remember Donaldson was Henry T. Brush's business partner at the time the creator of the Ransom Gillis House laid down on the floor of his study in 1879 and took his own life. John went on to become one of Detroit's first citizens. That is why mayor Maybury had asked him to add a letter to the Detroit Century Box discussing the current state of architecture in the city at the dawning of the 20th century. His letter to the future people of Detroit was entitled, "Rise of Architecture in Detroit" and opened with the following:

> *Standing upon the threshold of the 20th Century, it may not be without interest that we halt a brief moment to look back through the years of the 19th Century, so soon to close its doors forever. Were it possible for us to be carried back one hundred years and to look upon the village that then occupied the site of our present beautiful city, we should doubtless be filled with astonishment as great, as that of the resident of that then little town were he to awake from a century of sleep to look upon the city of today, and is it not altogether*

*probable that equally great if not greater progress will be made in the work of the next One hundred years?*[3]

Could Mr. Donaldson have imagined that in his beloved city 100 years later so many grand structures of the 19th century had been destroyed? Would he have believed us if we told him that much of the city had returned to a prairie-like setting inviting back long gone residents like red foxes and pheasants?[4] Would he have ever thought that so many of the magnificent structures in Detroit had been left abandoned for so long that urban spelunking of their interiors had become a local hobby? Imagine his horror in finding out that his city with all its wealth and potential at the close of the 19th century would in 2009 be so bankrupt that it could not even afford to bury the unclaimed dead in its morgue.[5] He could have not imagined how woefully wrong his hopes for 21st century Detroit were. And this leads us back to the question posed when I first saw the Ransom Gillis House that hot July afternoon in 2004 and begged it to tell me its story. We now know that story, but what has it taught us?

In an effort to answer this question and make some sense of all I had discovered about the history of the Ransom Gillis House, in September of 2006 I sought out Frank Rashid PhD, Chair, English and Modern Languages Department at Marygrove College in northwest Detroit. The tutor gothic style buildings at Marygrove, three stories high with steep slate tile roofs, produce an atmosphere that rivals any Ivy League campus. The grounds in which these buildings lay encompass over 50 acres, thick with old deciduous trees hiding the structures from the surrounding streets, streets of which felt like downtown Mogadishu as I drove through them. Enrollment at Marygrove at the time was only about 800. Approximately eighty percent of the students were Black and 80% of that female. The vast majority of the students came from Detroit proper. As I passed the guard gate I asked security if there was a charge for parking, his reply, "No, park anywhere you like."

Frank and I talked of Detroit and my research for over an hour and a half, quite an interesting time. Near the end of our talk I asked Frank, a lifetime resident of the City with a house near the University of Detroit, what could turn it around, he surprised me in stating, "Nothing, ... short of an ecological or political catastrophe that forced the remaining population to congregate within the city to be closer to central services."[6] The problems are just too big, the political will too small, and the general public's understanding of the underlying history seemingly non-existent. Thus, the current plan for urban renewal in Detroit consists of collision with a Near-Earth Asteroid and/or the onset of WWIII.

Undeterred I turned to another, yet untraditional, source for some enlightenment, my friend Shigeru, an electrical engineer that I have worked with for a number of years. Shig, as we call him, was a four year old living in the small coastal fishing town of Tokuyama when the bomb was dropped on Hiroshima less than 50 miles away. Some three and a half weeks later my own father, at the time a 20-year-old Navy Lookout stationed on the USS Idaho, found himself floating in Tokyo Bay as the Documents of Surrender were signed on the USS Missouri. Shig immigrated to Canada in adulthood and has lived and worked there and in the US ever since. We have had many a discussion of history, as we are both interested in such diversions. Upon discussing the Ransom Gillis House one day, he supplied me with his personal ideas on why Americans seem so unconcerned with history. I had always viewed this as one of our failings; Shig disagreed, politely of course. "America," he noted, "it a very interesting experiment. They try everything. Let's try this, maybe it work, OK. Europe and Asia different. They have new idea, then someone say, 'wait, wait, we try that 300 years ago, it not work good, we don't want to do that again.' American's, they

117

have short history, they look back and see not any mistake, so they try. Very interesting experiment this America!" Of course, our openness to try new ways of constructing our society, largely facilitated by an absence (or ignorance) of historical data, is quite a double-edged sword. But as Shig says, it does provide for an "interesting experiment." Alas I remained largely at a loss to understand the true dynamics of what brought the Detroit Metro area to its current state, something I sorely needed to grasp in order to finish this book. That all changed in May of 2009.

In May of 2009 my Dad, who still lived in the Detroit area, was diagnosed with an 11 cm aneurism in his ascending aorta. A significantly dangerous condition at any age. I spent most of the next 4 months back in the Detroit area, a place I had not spent more than a few weeks at a time in since I graduated college in 1983. I remained there helping my Dad through his surgery and recovery as well as getting him and my Mom moved out to Seattle. As I had spent my adult life outside the Detroit area, this much time being immersed in the local culture gave me a far better understanding of the dynamics that had brought it to its current state. I now began to understand how the Ransom Gillis House became what it became and what forced it in that direction. During the research for this book I continually looked for a simple smoking gun that would explain the state of the house I was so interested in, and that of the Detroit Metro area in general. When I was researching the chapter on the Blue Bloods, I continually searched for something somehow illustrating them as one of the original villains in this story. Try as I might, I could not find any facts to mount a case against them. Sure they were from well-established families in the New World and had an easier way to the top than the majority of the population, but there did not seem to be any real malice or greed in their actions. Yes, some of these actions would seem overly paternal by today's standards, but probably not so over 100 years ago.

True they greatly damaged the environment but this was not done with a real understanding of the ramifications of their actions and if they knew what we do now I am pretty convinced they would have seriously reconsidered. Environmentally they were not evil, they were just ignorant. Also by today's standards they were far closer connected to the average man than the rich are today. As my college aged daughter said when I took her by the house for the first time, "Hmm, that's not that big of a house!"

I had the same issue as I explored other stories connected with the house, many problems but not one big enough to account for the full catastrophe. Then I spent 4 months back in the Detroit area. Mind you my time there was spent in the working-class suburbs not Detroit proper. The first thing that hit me was the overwhelming impression I got that the people there had not fully grasped how far they had fallen and that they stubbornly clung to the belief that their current condition had its origins somewhere outside the area. They looked upon themselves as victims, illustrated by the bumper sticker I saw numerous times, "Out of a Job Yet? Keep Buying Foreign." The racial divide in the area was still primarily as it was when I was a child and this did not seem to disturb them to any great extent. And lastly, the people of the suburbs still thought that they were as separated economically from the City of Detroit as they were racially and demographically. This reinforced to me that the problems originate, as they always have, not just in Detroit proper but in the whole metro area. Slowly, painfully during the summer of 2009 I came to understand that the path the Detroit Metro area had followed to its current state had been paved by a unique culmination of a number of particularly virulent problems. I also came to the conclusion that the spread of Detroit's blight to the suburbs was eminent and unavoidable as the underlying causes were one in the same. I likened the issues that propelled southeastern Michigan into the state it is today to that of the many-

119

headed mythical Hydra of which Hercules fought. These many heads had to be tackled co-currently lest if you concentrate on just one the rest will devour you. In addition they all had to be handled properly so that two heads did not spring from the one just removed. And lastly, the final, immortal head had to be buried deep under a large stone such that it would never again be a danger. Now I do not profess to know how to best attack these heads, but what I do know is that before any attack can be mounted they must be revealed for what they are.

The first head is primarily of nature's making though understanding it and how the population reacted to it is critical. The first of these heads was the area's flat easily accessible landscape on three sides with water access facilitating low-density, single-family housing uniquely conducive to the automobile. This allowed convenient spoke-like road then freeway construction reinforcing the dominance of the car and single-family home. Lastly this easy access to buildable land provided people an escape from their problems instead of forcing them to stay put and work them out.

The next reptilian skull is one in which many the casual observer, especially from the outside, assumes is the major reason for the area's plight. This is of course the dominance and dependence on a single large manufacturing industry. Blaming everything on this one item is far too simplistic; especially when you consider that the origins and conditions in which this industry evolved were far more important than that it just produced one class of products. But the fact remains that the whole area has for 100 years been dependent on one industry and this industry has always been plagued by frequent boom and bust cycles.

The next head has close ties to the former, maybe so much so that you could say that they originated from the same stump. This is the fact that the automobile industry has for the majority of its life been uniquely dependent on unskilled or low-skilled labor. This fact was a great advantage to the people of the area in the years following WWII as it gave many of them their only real path to the middle class. Unfortunately, it also intensified racial tensions as unskilled workers both Black and White fought for the same low-skilled jobs on the factory floor.

With this as its base, the ugly head of racial prejudice made its presence known. The majority population, fearing the loss of their fragile grip on the middle-class, blamed their dilemma not on the industry they worked for or the economy of the country, but instead on those who looked most different from them. The first two of the Hydra's heads now allowed the Whites a way to physically separate themselves from the demons they had fabricated and they fled to the suburbs. But this was only a stopgap measure as their disease was not to be cured by simply moving 10 miles down the road. Unfortunately this did cause the City of Detroit to be slowly abandoned along with any chances of recovery of the Ransom Gillis House. But when the majority population and its associated capital fled the City this did not stop the devastation from eventually engulfing the surrounding metropolitan area. It only delayed it for a matter of time.

The next head is probably the most critical to this analysis as if it had been disposed of when it was young the domination of the beast over the whole metropolitan area could have been defeated. This is also the one that required my total immersion in the culture for four months to truly perceive, and the one that, in my opinion, will keep other industries from moving into the area for years to come. This most virulent and deadliest of the Hydra's heads can be best described as the "Entitlement Mentality." This assertion with all its obvious political and emotional baggage requires some explanation and validation to substantiate. Some blame this mentality on the dominance of unions but that is a simplistic answer as unions in the end only do what their membership

121

supports. Also unions in any industry can only survive if the industry itself survives. In the metastasization of the "Entitlement Mentality" the union membership, the auto giants, as well as the general public were all equally complicit. Unions were originally critical institutions to enable the creation of a middle class in the US. They were also not always as apathetic of the economics the companies they worked for had to face. "As early as the 1940s, UAW president Walter Reuther was urging the auto companies to produce small, inexpensive cars for the average American. In 1947 and '48 the union even offered to cut wages if the Big Three would reduce the price of their cars."[7] The living wage provided to the autoworker and the taxes paid by the factories allowed working-class cities throughout the Detroit area to provide a world-class public education to their children. Something their parents never had the opportunity to enjoy. Unfortunately, in many cases this gift of a quality public education was squandered. Throughout the 1970's and early eighties the children of WWII and Korean War veterans entered the workforce. Unfortunately Detroit still dominated the auto industry, holding over 80% of the market.[8] This monopoly was intensified by the manner in which auto companies negotiated their contracts with their major supplier of labor the UAW. Basically the UAW would choose, on a revolving basis, one of the auto giants to negotiate with, or strike. Once this first settlement was reached the other companies, dealing primarily with the same UAW, would follow suit. This monopoly allowed workers in the auto industry to claim higher wages than equivalent jobs, if ones even existed, in other unrelated industries. The US auto giants had no competition thus they could give out these generous pay and compensation packages essentially passing the cost onto the general American public. From the 1980's to the dawning of the 21$^{st}$ century this resulted in wages, healthcare benefits, and retirement programs that far exceeded those of similar jobs throughout the country. By the first decade of the 21$^{st}$ century US autoworkers were costing the company $74/hour when the same worker at a Japanese plant in the US was costing about $50. All this while the actual pay rate for workers in both plants was about the same. The difference here being the generous health care and pension plans the UAW had won earlier. By 2008 these "legacy costs" would add about $2000 or more to the cost of each car.[9]

One of the most egregious programs to come out of the deals made between the automakers and the UAW in the 1980's was the Job Bank.

> *The 'Jobs Banks' program was created in 1984 when the Big Three automakers struck a deal with the United Auto Workers (UAW) to provide security for those displaced by automation and modernization of manufacturing processes. Under the program laid-off workers can collect up to full pay by participating in the jobs banks, where they have the option of performing community service or doing nothing at all. At the program's height in 2006, nearly 15,000 people took part in the jobs banks, many of them getting full pay while not performing any duties for the automakers.[10]*

Obviously policies like this are seen as ludicrous outside the auto industry as they simply negate any efficiencies obtained by automation. But at the time these agreements were made the monopoly present allowed these costs to be passed onto the final purchaser of the car. Of course as Japanese and other manufacturers slowly entered the US market (and Americans throughout the nation realized they were not getting their money's worth buying from the Big 3) these types of programs and contracts became less and less sustainable. Unfortunately both the companies and the union were far to slow to notice and react to these changing dynamics. They had always gotten these perks; there was no reason why they should not continue to get them.

The worst legacy of this though was that the availability of high paying, high security, high pension jobs deterred a great number of the area's population from developing skills that were marketable in industries and areas outside of southeastern Michigan. But as the US auto manufacture's market share slowly ebbed away the companies and their workers arrogantly clung to their old ways expecting them to continue ad infinitum. Of course this could never be, so now you are left, at the close of the first decade of the 21$^{st}$ century, with 50 year old men, possessing only a high school education, use to living off a 6-figure income which has now evaporated, and after years in the workforce possessing only the marketable skills to earn a fraction of what they once did. This adds a critical dampening effect to the renewal of manufacturing of any type in the area. Knowing the history of labor/management relationships over the last 30 years if you were a company would you risk investing huge sums of capital in an area not knowing when the union's virile Hydra's head would again spawn from the bellies of the local population?

This most deadly of the Hydra's weapons unfortunately led to the growth of a related one that became firmly entrenched in the area's fabric. As the autoworkers won larger and larger benefits other parts of the Detroit Metro economy followed suit if they could. This was fairly easy for related industries like steel production but at least these businesses would ultimately be curtailed by economics. A much bigger danger arose when local governments grew due to their stable, lucrative industrial tax base and their public employees started requesting and getting these types of benefits. When the auto industry had its monopoly the taxes it supplied made this sustainable, once it ebbed it was not. Unfortunately public entities are usually the slowest to respond and will sometimes do so only as a last resort. This became blatantly obvious to me on a trip to the local bank in my hometown of Trenton a 20-minute drive from the Ransom Gillis House. I had gone there with my Dad to transfer his accounts to a bank in the Seattle area. During a conversation with the banker we casually started talking about housing prices in my hometown. I learned that she, the person helping us, had attempted to purchase a house in Trenton a year or so earlier, but was thwarted as she found out that the property taxes on her new purchase would be higher than her mortgage payment! This startled me, and after doing some crude math I came up with the fact that the property taxes in my hometown were 5 times that of which I pay in suburban Seattle. Admittedly the public services as I remember them were much better in my hometown than here in Seattle, but they were not THAT much better!

This experience motivated me to look a little closer at the tax burden in the Detroit Metro area compared to that in the Seattle area. I had always believed that the tax structure in Washington State was regressive as sales taxes not income taxes are one of the major bases of state funding. I also knew that the taxes back East were higher than in Washington State but I really did not know to what extent. After a little research the results I came up with surprised me but also helped explain the plight of urban southeastern Michigan. In the 2007 study "Tax Rates and Tax Burdens in the District of Columbia -A Nationwide Comparison" an evaluation was done on the overall tax burden in the largest city in each state plus the District of Columbia. This study looked at the overall tax burden of a typical family of three at annual income levels of $25,000, $50,000, $75,000, $100,000, and $150,000. The results given there were surprising even to me. The results below are out of 51 cities of course.

- At income level of $25,000/yr Detroit had the 16th highest tax burden while Seattle had the 26th.
- At income level of $50,000/yr Detroit had the 3rd highest tax burden while Seattle had the 48th.
- At income level of $75,000/yr Detroit had the 4th highest tax burden while Seattle had the 48th.

- At income level of $100,000/yr Detroit had the 4th highest tax burden while Seattle had the 47th.
- At income level of $150,000/yr Detroit had the 4th highest tax burden while Seattle had the 48th.
- Looking at all income brackets Detroit had the 4th highest tax burden while Seattle had the 48th.[11]

It should be noted that the numbers for the $25,000 data point have limited validity as they assume that the property taxes paid in Detroit and Seattle are the same due to the fact that at this income level most of the families are renters not owners of homes. Because the property taxes in Detroit are so high and those in Seattle so low this makes the burden spread between the two cities at that income level in this study far closer than it actually is. Since property taxes are typically implemented to reduce the burden on elderly long-term residents at the cost of young families, the high tax burden in the Detroit Metro area actually deters new, young families from moving in. As a result in my hometown of Trenton the median age is 42 while that in the US is 35.[12] It seems though that Trenton, as with may other cities in the area, ignored obvious signs that economic conditions were changing such that their tax structure was unsustainable. As the industrial base in Trenton (a steel mill, engine plant, and chemical plant) slowly shrunk over the last 30 years so did the taxes they paid. This occurred slowly; slow enough so that it was politically viable to ignore it. Fire, police, and other City functions continued to expand with their associated legacy costs as politicians found it difficult to curtail city services. It was far more politically palatable to increase property taxes on the newer families than the older ones as the latter dominated the voting base. Of course this was a self-fulfilling prophecy bringing them to the point were it is now not economically feasible for younger families, the future of course, to move into the city.

Intensified by the housing bubble burst of 2008-2009 and the collapse of the auto industry, Trenton as with the

whole Detroit Metro area saw people leaving in droves sometimes abandoning their houses behind them. Of course the
City of Trenton's response to such events was predictably dra-
conian. In June of 2009 the Trenton City Council passed an
ordinance supposedly to prevent blight. I became aware of
this when I went to city hall to change my parent's house to a
rental. During that time I overheard one of the city employees
telling a person on the phone, "Well you know we have had a
lot of problems with that property." Inquiring about the conversation I overheard a staff member proudly boasted about
the new ordinance the council had just passed entitled, "Vacant Property Registration and Maintenance." The ordinance
read:

> *The purpose of establishing a registration process for vacant*
> *properties is to provide requirements for responsible parties*
> *to implement the required vacant property maintenance plan*
> *for such properties which will protect public health, safety*
> *and general welfare of the citizens and prevent neighborhood*
> *blight, ensure properties are secured, prevent deterioration,*
> *and protect property values and neighborhood integrity.*[13]

And required,

> *Owners and/or owners' agents of real property are required*
> *to register all vacant property within 30 days of the vacancy*
> *or the effective date of this ordinance whichever is later. Reg-*
> *istration pursuant to this section shall be renewed annu-*
> *ally.*[14]

Among other things the ordinance requires,

1. *perform regular weekly inspections of the property to assure*
   *compliance with the requirements of this section.*
2. *Weeds shall be removed from landscape beds, the perimeter*

*of buildings, along fence lines, and in parking lot joints and*
*cracks.*

3. *Grass height shall be maintained no higher than 12 inches*
   *and the trimmings removed from the property.*
4. *Building appurtenances must be securely attached so as not*
   *to cause a blighting condition, including, but not limited to,*
   *gutters, downspouts, shutters, railings, guards, steps,*
   *awnings, canopies, signs, light fixtures, and fire-escapes.*[15]

If this was not done then,

> *The building official or his or her designee shall have the*
> *authority to require the owner to implement additional*
> *maintenance, security, or other measures not specified in the*
> *vacant property maintenance plan, as may be reasonably re-*
> *quired to prevent further decline.*[16]

With the costs assessed to the owner I assume. And if you do
not do this then,

> *Any owner of vacant property that fails to register, fails to*
> *report changes to registration information, or fails to renew*
> *a registration annually shall be responsible for a civil infrac-*
> *tion and assessed a fine in an amount established from time*
> *to time by resolution of the city council. Any owner or*
> *owner's agent of vacant property subject to the registration*
> *requirements of this division, and causes, permits, or main-*
> *tains a violation of this division as to that property, shall be*
> *responsible for a civil infraction.*[17]

In a nutshell instead of addressing the core issues causing the
abandonment of houses in the city of Trenton they were simply going to solve the problem by passing a law against it!
Considering the age demographics in the city and the fact that
dead people are usually not very reliable in maintaining their

houses, the city has set itself up to become an owner of structures and land that are and will continue to plummet in value. A circumstance that started Detroit proper down the path some 30 years ago to becoming the major city with the most vacant land in the country. Yet with this example only 15 miles away the residents of my hometown seem oblivious.

Another example of the oppressive weight of the public institutions in the area and their unresponsiveness to the realities occurring around them was a water rate hike proposed by the Detroit Water Department in the summer of 2009. The Detroit Water Department supplies fresh water not only to the City but also to the majority of the surrounding suburbs. Pulling their supply from huge pipes out in Lake Huron far to the north, the water system is one of the largest in the nation. So what was the reason they gave for raising water rates? People were conserving too much water![18] Whereas when all the rest of the communities on the planet Earth are going to great lengths to encourage their populations to conserve this precious resource of fresh water, the Detroit Water Department was doing exactly the opposite. The organization had gotten so big and disconnected from the outside economy that the product they supplied no longer had any connection to how much of it was actually needed by their customers. Worse yet, there was no real public outcry over such an announcement. Sure it was a small story in the Detroit Free Press and on the local nightly news but there was no astonishment in the words of the reporters or from the public to which they were addressing. The underlying absurdity of the whole situation seemed to be lost on them, or perhaps they had just grown numb from exposure to such inconsistencies for decades.

I can only assume similar examples are present throughout the Detroit Metro area and gives credence to the idea that the problems are not limited to Detroit but involve the environment in all of urban southeastern Michigan.

Like the final immortal head of which Hercules could not kill by cauterizing its stump, this "entitlement mentality" will be the most difficult for the area to cope with and will require a very large boulder on top of it to ensure it does not make a reappearance. That is if and when it can actually be placed under that weight.

As this dangerous multi-headed daemon continues to wreak havoc in the Detroit Metropolitan Area, the young, the educated, the future, will continue to come to the conclusion that battling it is in vain. As these people leave the area, "Michigan gets less populated, less educated, and poorer because of Outmigration... It's a vicious downward cycle; the best and brightest leave; entrepreneurs don't come to the state because the best and brightest are elsewhere; as more people leave, that leaves fewer people to pay for services. Neither one will make Michigan a very appealing place."[19]  Even though Michigan still has some of the best universities in the nation if not the world over half the in-state graduates of University of Michigan leave the state upon graduation. The numbers are similar for schools throughout the state and of these who do leave the vast majority think they will never come back.[20] Thus the trend towards a smaller population dominated by an older, less educated, and poorer demographic in southeastern Michigan seems inevitable. The "Brain Drain" will be like that seen in a Third World country after a *coup d'état*. The population will increase its dangerous skewing to the elderly until there will be no way their pensions and medical costs can be sustained by the local population. This will end in a drastic reduction in the standard of living for all in the area. If the people of the area do this proactively the resulting pain could be minimized, but be there no delusions it will occur either BY THEM or TO THEM by forces outside their control.

How to stop this degradation I do not know, that is why I left the area almost 30 years ago. Hopefully some of this historical data surrounding the life and times of the Ransom

Gillis House will provide some insight to those far smarter than I in their attempt to stem the tide. What I do know though is that the solution must come from the people of the Detroit Metro area itself and it needs the participation of the entire area not just those within the borders of the City of Detroit. The general population of southeastern Michigan through their actions, reactions, or lack of action to situations presented to them created the problems they face today and only they can solve them.

More troubling for those of us on the outside is the knowledge that the elements of this Hydra are present in many of our cities and communities in varying numbers and intensities. It just so happens that they were all present in the Detroit Metro area and were intensely vicious. Maybe the true value of this story is the lessons the rest of us can learn from it. Some believe that the rise and fall of neighborhoods, cities, nations, and even civilizations are inevitable natural cycles that cannot be avoided. I do not believe this needs to be the case if we approach history as we do other aspects of the world around us. In the middle ages the people of Europe thought that periodic visits of the Black Death were inevitable. We now know this not to be the case. By understanding the causes of the plague through logical use of the scientific method we were able to stop these periodic visits and the devastation of large swaths of the population that in turn tore at the very fabric of the culture itself. Proper understanding of the experiences in Detroit can help us in this same way.

In the final analysis the house at the corner of John R and Alfred Street, which looks like it would be more comfortable on the Acropolis of Athens than in a major American City, serves us best as a warning, an alarm bell so to speak, to caution us not to repeat the mistakes that led to its demise.

Perhaps this work is its final eulogy.

# le détroit (The Straits)

### With apologies to Mr. Poe

*Once I found myself residing, like a train upon a siding,*
*In a place I was assured I had been many times before ---*
*Sitting there did I ponder, yes my mind it did then wander,*
*What is this place for which I have a memory store?*
*What hold on me does this place have I do implore?*
*Tis a dream, nothing more.*

*Passing memories though they are fleeting, alas they bear a quick repeating,*
*So that the lessons learned before us do not fall like dust upon the floor ---*
*This place it has a storied past, perhaps it just grew too fast?*
*Creating problems from which the social fabric tore,*
*Till simply living became so much a chore.*
*But I am a guest here, nothing more.*

*In a land divided such, the close observer can learn much,*
*If one treats as equal the stories told by both King and whore ---*
*In a place where workers ruled, provided that their voice was pooled,*
*They came from the South and every distant shore,*
*With their lives upon their backs, into The Straits did they pour,*
*Perhaps this was the problem, nothing more.*

*Steel, rubber, gasoline, soon black soot was all that could be seen,*
*From the Gothic structures where the lumber barons once did roar ---*
*These Patriarchs were first to flee, to the suburbs which held the key,*
*To a way of life away from thee whom they deplore,*
*Though these workers their yoke they still did bore.*
*Small concern, nothing more.*

*Left behind the peasants fought, forgetting all their Good Book taught,*
*Battling with one another for that job upon the factory floor ---*
*To determine who worthy was, where they could live and what one does,*
*You simply looked upon the color which their skin bore,*
*Yes, just the pigment that they wore.*
*Fear and hatred, nothing more.*

*From the time of Eighteen Sixty Three, the amount of melanin inside thee,*
*Set the load and burden one must shore ---*
*Then came Nineteen fifty-six, the Highway Act entered the mix,*
*Providing Whites the escape they had not had before,*
*So into the suburbs they did pour.*
*I tell you facts, nothing more.*

*In a house divided thus, from the past to learn you must,*
*Solutions there are present if one cares but to explore ---*
*To the Heavens look some might, but History will give you clearer sight,*
*Look there for hope I do implore,*
*Look there for a way outside this door.*
*But these are mere words, nothing more.*

*Pain and suffering and Urban blight, I do wonder is there light?*
*Upon the place where Cadillac first came ashore ---*
*Being gone now decades three, though I am not one of thee,*
*Luck I wish you in your Herculean chore,*
*As it is yours to bear, it is yours to shore.*
*I return here, Nevermore.*

# Index

## H

Hamid II, Abdul · 64, 65
Harpers Ferry · 38, 39
Hastings Street · 77, 85
Heffron, Daniel · 41
Heston, Charlton · 113
Hillsdale College · vii, 15, 16
Hiroshima · 117
Home Mission Society · 48, 49, 50
Hydra · 85, 86, 88, 115, 120, 121, 124, 131
Hypo · 26

## I

I-75 · 77, 85, 107
Immigrants · 28
Irish · 13
Iron · 81

## J

Jackson, Stonewall · 38
Japanese · 123
Jefferson · 15, 84
Jefferson Avenue · 15, 84
Jersey City · 30
Jews · 65
Job Bank · 123
John R · 1, 3, 4, 8, 9, 17, 28, 29, 34, 44, 51, 52, 67, 71, 72, 75, 77, 81, 92, 96, 99, 102, 110, 112, 113, 131
Johnson, Mike · 97
Jones, Bishop Rosa · 90
Josar, David · 105

## K

Kahn, Albert · 17
Kalamazoo College · 44

Kennedy, John F. · 80
Kessler, William · 96
Kilpatrick, Kwame · 111
King, Steven · 7
Kirk, Mike · vii, 100
Ku Klux Klan · 74
Kurdish · 67
Kurds · 63, 68
Kuykendall, Douglas · vii, 102, 103, 104, 105, 106, 107, 110, 113

## L

L.A. · 25, 26, 30
Lafayette Street · 13
Lake Michigan · 40, 42
Lawrence Tech · 95
Lodgers · 60
Los Angeles · 25, 26, 30
Lumber Barons · 42, 43

## M

Machu Picchu · 4, 5
Mack · 83
Manestique River · 40
Manistique & Northwestern Railway · 41
Manistique, MI · vii, 34, 40, 41, 42, 43, 44, 51
Mardirosian, Mark · 100
Marygrove College · vii, 116
Mason, George · 8, 9, 17, 18, 29, 60
Mathematical Instruments · 12
Maybury, William C. · 115
McKinley, William · 46
McLauchlin, Russell · 52, 53, 63, 73
Melchers, Gari · 19
Methodist Church · 15
Mexico · 45, 68, 70

# Y

# Z

# Notes

## Chapter 1

[1] "8 Mile," (2002), Universal Pictures (USA).

[2] "Blade Runner," (1982), Warner Brothers (USA), Blade Runner is the best and one of the most influential Science Fiction films ever made. Based on the excellent book "Do Androids Dream of Electric Sheep", by Philip K. Dick, Ridley Scott created Blade Runner as a stunning view of the dark near-future. Although seen as disturbingly bleak when it was first released, as time has moved on, it can now be seen as increasingly prophetic of the way the world is changing.
[http://www.brmovie.com/What_is_BR.htm] (6/15/2005)

[3] Ransom Gillis Home, University of Michigan,
[http://detroit1701.psc.isr.umich.edu./RansomGillisHome.html] (8/14/2004).

[4] Four Brothers, Paramount Pictures,
[http://www.fourbrothersmovie.com/home.html] (11/28/2008)

[5] Ed Vulliamy, Troops 'vandalize' ancient city of Ur, May 18, 2003, The Observer,
[http://observer.guardian.co.uk/international/story/0,6903,958429,00.html]
(10/4/2005)

[6] Charlemagne, Wikipedia [http://en.wikipedia.org/wiki/Charlemagne]
(11/28/2008)

[7] For an excellent review of the latest research on Pre-Columbian populations in the Americas see: Mann, Charles C. 1491: New Revelations of the Americas Before Columbus. New York: Knopf, 2005.

[8] King, Steven. The Stand. Doubleday, 1978

[9] Mann, Charles C. 1491: New Revelations of the Americas Before Columbus. New York: Knopf, 2005. P. 56.

[10] Ransom Gillis House - Brush Park Ruins, [http://detroityes.com/gild/01bp-gillis.htm] (8/2004)

[11] Ransom Gillis Home, University of Michigan,
[http://detroit1701.psc.isr.umich.edu./RansomGillisHome.html] (8/14/2004).

[12] Kidorf, Kristine. "RE: Ransom Gillis Home." E-mail to John Kossik. Aug. 19, 2004.

## Chapter 2

[1] "Horrible Suicide," The Evening News, Detroit Tuesday July 15, 1879, 4 O'clock Edition

[2] HeritageQuest Online – Census Image, 1860 Census, Michigan, Wayne, 5-WD Detroit, Series: M653, Roll: 565, Page: 468 [http://persi.heritagequestonline.com]
(7/6/;2005)

[3] Ibid

[4] William Austin Burt, [http://www.geo.msu.edu/geo333/burt.html](7/8/2005)

[5] W-M, Obelisk, [http://www.world-mysteries.com/alignments/mpl_al3a.htm](7/9/2005)

[6] Jacobs, Lisa D. E-mail to John Kossik, 7/8/2005. From Charles E. Smart's book The Makers of Surveying Instruments in America Since 1700 (Troy: Regal Art Press, 1962, p. 51-52), originally quoted from Detroit Advertiser 10/23/1858.

[7] Grant & Crosman, [http://www.surveyhistory.org/grant_&_crosman.htm]
(7/6/2005)

[8] Websters Instrument Makers Database – Letter G, page 54 of 79,
[http://www.aklerplanetarium.org/history/websters/g.htm](7/6/2005)

[9] Grant & Crosman,
[http://www.surveyhistory.org/grant_&_crosman.htm](7/6/2005)
[10] Clark, Charles F. Charles F. Clark's annual directory of the inhabitants, incorporated companies, business firms, &c. of the city of Detroit for 1865-'6, Detroit C.F. Clark, 1865, p.103, HeritageQuest Online – Books Image,
[http://persi.heritagequestonline.com] (7/3/2005)
[11] The Michigan Manual, Legislative Service Bureau (Michigan), August 1993, pp. 22-23.
[12] Conot, Robert, American Odyssey, Wayne State University Press, Detroit, 1986, p. 74.
[13] A Thrilling Narrative From the Lips of the Sufferers of the Late Detroit Riot, March 6, 1863, with the Hair breadth Escapes of Men, Women and Children, and Destruction of Colored Men's Property, Not Less Than $15,000. Detroit Michigan, 1863, No Author
[http://docsouth.unc.edu/neh/detroit/detroit.html] (5/1/2005)
[14] Ibid, p. 23-24.
[15] Clark, Charles F. Charles F. Clark's annual directory of the inhabitants, incorporated companies, business firms, &c. of the city of Detroit for 1865-'6, Detroit C.F. Clark, 1865, p.103, HeritageQuest Online – Books Image,
[http://persi.heritagequestonline.com] (7/3/2005)
[16] Clark, Charles F. Charles F. Clark's annual directory of the inhabitants, business firms, incorporated companies, etc. of the city of Detroit for 1868-9, Detroit C.F. Clark, 1868, p.117, HeritageQuest Online – Books Image,
[http://persi.heritagequestonline.com] (7/2/2005)
[17] Clark, Charles F. Charles F. Clark's annual directory of the inhabitants, business firms, incorporated companies, etc. of the city of Detroit for 1869-70, Detroit C.F. Clark, 1869, p.135, HeritageQuest Online – Books Image,
[http://persi.heritagequestonline.com] (7/2/2005)
[18] Anonymous, Hubbell & Weeks' annual city directory of the inhabitants, business firms, incorporated companies, etc. of the city of Detroit, for 1872-3, Detroit: Hubbell & Weeks, 1872, p. 161, HeritageQuest Online – Books Image,
[http://persi.heritagequestonline.com] (7/2/2005)
[19] King, Donald L. "HT Brush." E-mail to John Kossik. May 9, 2005.
[20] Crause, Andrew, Photo from Woodmere Cemetery, 3/28/2005.
[21] Anonymous, J.W. Weeks& Co.'s annual city directory of the inhabitants, business firms, incorporated companies, etc. of the city of Detroit, for 1873-4, Detroit: J.W. Weeks, 1873, p. 176, HeritageQuest Online – Books Image,
[http://persi.heritagequestonline.com] (7/2/2005)
[22] Anonymous, J.W. Weeks& Co.'s annual city directory of the inhabitants, business firms, incorporated companies, etc. of the city of Detroit, for 1874-5, Detroit: J.W. Weeks, 1874, p. 169, HeritageQuest Online – Books Image,
[http://persi.heritagequestonline.com] (7/2/2005)
[23] HeritageQuest Online – Census Image, 1870 Census, Michigan, Wayne, 5-WD Detroit, Series: M593, Roll: 712, Page: 305 [http://persi.heritagequestonline.com] (7/6/2005)
[24] Crause, Andrew, Photo from Woodmere Cemetery, 3/28/2005.
[25] Suitor, Stephanie . "Methodist Church pre-1879." E-mail to John Kossik. Tue 5/10/2005.
[26] J.W. Weeks & Co., Detroit city directory for 1879 : embracing a complete alphabetical list of business firms and private citizens, a directory of the city and county officers, churches, public and private schools, benevolent, literary, and other associations, banks and incorporated institutions : to which is added a complete classified business directory of Detroit Detroit: J.W. Weeks & Co., 1879, 922 pgs.
[http://www.heritagequestonline.com/prod/genealogy/fullcitation?docID=Genealogy-glh40846386] (8/30/2004)

[27] Wright, Robert. "Other Brush Structures." E-mail to John Kossik. 7/27/2005.

[28] Cangany, Catherine. "Henry T. Brush." E-mail to John Kossik. May 9, 2005.

[29] J.W. Weeks & Co., Detroit city directory for 1879 : embracing a complete alphabetical list of business firms and private citizens, a directory of the city and county officers, churches, public and private schools, benevolent, literary, and other associations, banks and incorporated institutions : to which is added a complete classified business directory of Detroit Detroit: J.W. Weeks & Co., 1879, 922 pgs. [http://www.heritagequestonline.com/prod/genealogy/fullcitation?docID=Genealogy-glh40846386] (8/30/2004)

[30] Eckert, Kathryn, B. "Buildings of Michigan." Oxford University Press, New York, 1993, p. 199.

[31] Michigan Registered Historic Site Marker, Orchard Lake Chapel, Orchard Lake Michigan, Michigan History Division, Department of State, Registered local Site No. 284, Property of the State of Michigan, 1974.

[32] 1870 U.S. Census, MICHIGAN, WAYNE, 5-WD DETROIT, Age: 60, Male, Race: WHITE, Born: SCOT, Series: M593 Roll: 712 Page: 239 [http://persi.heritagequestonline.com.access-proxy.sno-isle.org/hqoweb/library/do/census/results/image/download?urn=urn%3Aproquest%3AUS%3Bcensus%3B1781723%3B7140439%3B9%3B9&searchtype=1&offset=0&filename=/heritage/vault/hqc45/M593/712/1/239B.tif&invert=0&scale=2&mimeType=application/pdf&saveAs=1] (4/5/2010)

[33] Cangany, Catherine. "Henry T. Brush." E-mail to John Kossik. May 9, 2005.

[34] King, Donald L. "Re: HT Brush." E-mail to John Kossik. May 10, 2005.

[35] Cangany, Catherine. "RE: HT Brush." E-mail to John Kossik. May 10, 2005.

[36] Treasurers Annual Report, Hillsdale College, June 15, 1874, Moore, Linda. "RE: Central Hall." E-mail to John Kossik. June 28, 2005.

[37] Jones, David H. "Letter to John Kossik," May 12, 2005.

[38] J.W. Weeks & Co., Detroit city directory for 1879 : embracing a complete alphabetical list of business firms and private citizens, a directory of the city and county officers, churches, public and private schools, benevolent, literary, and other associations, banks and incorporated institutions : to which is added a complete classified business directory of Detroit Detroit: J.W. Weeks & Co., 1879, 922 pgs. [http://www.heritagequestonline.com/prod/genealogy/fullcitation?docID=Genealogy-glh40846386] (8/30/2004)

[39] Farmer, Silas. The History of Detroit and Michigan, or, The metropolis illustrated : chronology cyclopaedia of the past and present : including a full record of territorial days in Michigan and the annals of Wayne County. Detroit. S. Farmer & Co. 1884. p. 760.

[40] Ferry, W. H. The Buildings of Detroit: A History. Wayne State University Press. Detroit. 1980. p. 90.

[41] Ibid p. 86.

[42] Albert Kahn Associates, Inc. History. [http://www.albertkahn.com/cmpny_history.cfm] (2/18/2005)

[43] Links, J.G. Ed. Ruskin, John. The Stones of Venice. Hill and Wang. New York. 1960. p. 113.

[44] Ferry, W. H. The Buildings of Detroit: A History. Wayne State University Press. Detroit. 1980. p. 83.

[45] Ransom Gillis Home, University of Michigan, [http://detroit1701.psc.isr.umich.edu./RansomGillisHome.html] (8/14/2004).

[46] Details of original configuration of the Ransom Gillis Home from current photographs by John Kossik of the structure and "Picture of Ransom Gillis Home." Burton Historical Collection.

[47] For an example of Victorian house plans of the period see: Bicknell, A.J., Comstock, W.T., Victorian Architecture: Two Pattern Books, The American Life Foundation& Study Institute, Watkins Glen, New York, 1976.

[48] Conot, Robert, American Odyssey, Wayne State University Press, Detroit, 1986, p. 50.

[49] Kuykendall, Douglas. Personal conversation with John Kossik, 6/3/2005.

[50] J.W. Weeks & Co., Detroit city directory for 1879 : embracing a complete alphabetical list of business firms and private citizens, a directory of the city and county officers, churches, public and private schools, benevolent, literary, and other associations, banks and incorporated institutions : to which is added a complete classified business directory of Detroit Detroit: J.W. Weeks & Co., 1879, 922 pgs.
[http://www.heritagequestonline.com/prod/genealogy/fullcitation?docID=Genealogy-glh40846386] (8/30/2004)

[51] Weeks, Harriet Morse, Descendants of Richard Hayes : of Lyme, Connecticut, through his son Titus Hayes, Pittsfield, Mass.: Eagle Pub. Co., 1904, 192 pgs.
[http://www.heritagequestonline.com/prod/genealogy/fullcitation?docID=Genealogy-glh11872914] (8/30/2004)

[52] Marquis, Albert Nelson, The Book of Detroiters : a biographical dictionary of leading living men of the city of Detroit, Chicago: A.N. Marquis & Co., 1908, 496 pgs.
[http://www.heritagequestonline.com/prod/genealogy/fullcitation?docID=Genealogy-glh20904590] (9/10/2004)

[53] Ross, Robert, B. Landmarks of Detroit: a history of the city. Evening News Association. Detroit. 1898. p. 171. [http://persi.haritagequestonline.com/] (10/14/2004)

[54] Donaldson, John M. John M .Donaldson papers, 1873-1938. microfilm copy. Archives of American Art, Smithsonian Institution, Washington, D.C. 20560

[55] War Department Weather Map, Washington, Monday, July, 14 1879 ---- 7:35 A.M., Signal Service U.S. Army, Division of Telegrams and Reports for the Benefit of Commerce and Agriculture.
[http://docs.lib.noaa.gov/rescue/dwm/data_rescue_daily_weather_maps.html] (6/24/2005)

[56] Singer, Christopher M. "In service to Detroit." The Detroit News, 21 May 2001, [http://www.detnews.com/2001/detroit/0103/21/s06-201842.htm] (6/24/2005)

[57] "The Late Henry T. Brush," The Evening News, Detroit Tuesday July 15, 1879, 5 O'clock Edition.

[58] The Sanborn Map Company, Sanborn Library, LLC,
[http://sanborn.umi.com/sanborn/image/download/pdf/mi/reel07/3985/00006/Detroit+1884-1899+vol.+1%2C+1884%2+Sheet+2_b.pdf] (6/24/2005)

[59] Weeks & Co. Detroit city directory for 1879 , Detroit: J.W. Weeks & Co., 1879, 922 pgs.
[http://persi.heritagequestonline.com/hqoweb/library/do/books/results/image?urn=urn%3Aproquest%3AUS%3Bglhbooks%3BGenealogy-glh40846386%3B8%3B-1%3B&polarity=&scale=&jumptophysicalpage=152]

[60] The Sanborn Map Company, Sanborn Library, LLC,
[http://sanborn.umi.com/sanborn/image/download/pdf/mi/reel07/3985/00081/Detroit+1884-1899+vol.+2%2C+1884%2C+Sheet+39_a.pdf]

[61] "The Late Henry T. Brush," The Evening News, Detroit Tuesday July 15, 1879, 5 O'clock Edition.

[62] Ibid.

[63] War Department Weather Map, Washington, Monday, July, 14 1879 ---- 7:35 A.M., Signal Service U.S. Army, Division of Telegrams and Reports for the Benefit of Commerce and Agriculture.
[http://docs.lib.noaa.gov/rescue/dwm/data_rescue_daily_weather_maps.html] (6/24/2005)

[64] "Horrible Suicide," The Evening News, Detroit Tuesday July 15, 1879, 4 O'clock Edition.

[65] "The Dead Architect," Detroit Free Press. Thursday July 17, 1879, Page 1.

[66] War Department Weather Map, Washington, Tuesday, July, 15 1879 ---- 4:35 P.M., Signal Service U.S. Army, Division of Telegrams and Reports for the Benefit of Commerce and Agriculture.

[67] "The Dead Architect," Detroit Free Press. Thursday July 17, 1879, Page 1.

[68] "Horrible Suicide," The Evening News, Detroit Tuesday July 15, 1879, 4 O'clock Edition.

[69] Ibid

[70] "The Dead Architect," Detroit Free Press. Thursday July 17, 1879, Page 1.

[71] Clark, Charles F. Charles F. Clark's annual directory of the inhabitants, incorporated companies, business firms, &c., of the city of Detroit for 1865-'6. Detroit: C.F. Clark, 1865, p. 152 [http://persi.heritagewuestonline.com/] (7/3/2005)

[72] War Department Weather Map, Washington, Monday, July, 17 1879 ---- 4:35 P.M., Signal Service U.S. Army, Division of Telegrams and Reports for the Benefit of Commerce and Agriculture.
[http://docs.lib.noaa.gov/rescue/dwm/data_rescue_daily_weather_maps.html] (6/24/2005)

[73] Detroit city directory for 1879, Detroit: J.W. Weeks & Co., 1879, 922 pgs., page 33.
[http://persi.heritagequestonline.com/hqoweb/library/do/books/results/image?ur n=urn%3Aproquest%3AUS%3Bglhbooks%3BGenealogy-glh40846386%3B3%3B-1%3B&polarity=&scale=&jumptophysicalpage=33](3/6/2005)

[74] Crause, Andrew, Photo from Woodmere Cemetery, 3/28/2005.

[75] J.W. Weeks & Co., Detroit city directory for 1879 : embracing a complete alphabetical list of business firms and private citizens, a directory of the city and county officers, churches, public and private schools, benevolent, literary, and other associations, banks and incorporated institutions : to which is added a complete classified business directory of Detroit Detroit: J.W. Weeks & Co., 1879, 922 pgs.
[http://www.heritagequestonline.com/prod/genealogy/fullcitation?docID=Genealo gy-glh40846386] (8/30/2004) p. 369.

[76] Crause, Andrew, Photo from Woodmere Cemetery, 3/28/2005.

[77] Marquis, Albert Nelson, Ed. The Book of Detroiter: A Biographical Dictionary of Leading Living Men of the City of Detroit. Chicago: A.N. Marquis & Company, Chicago, 1908, p. 143-146.
[http://www.usgennet.org/usa/mi/county/Tuscola/det/detdod-dou.htm] (8/16/2004).

[78] Weeks, Harriet Morse, Descendants of Richard Hayes : of Lyme, Connecticut, through his son Titus Hayes, Pittsfield, Mass.: Eagle Pub. Co., 1904, 192 pgs.
[http://www.heritagequestonline.com/prod/genealogy/fullcitation?docID=Genealo gy-glh11872914] (8/30/2004)

[79] The Blue book of Detroit and suburbs : a social directory : forming a convenient guide for calls and parties, and a select list for mailing purposes.Detroit, Mich.: Blue Book Pub. Co., c1893, 226 pgs.
[http://www.heritagequestonline.com/prod/genealogy/fullcitation?docID=Genealo gy-glh20906399] (8/31/2004)

[80] Marquis, Albert Nelson, The Book of Detroiters : a biographical dictionary of leading living men of the city of Detroit, Chicago: A.N. Marquis & Co., 1908, 496 pgs.
[http://www.heritagequestonline.com/prod/genealogy/fullcitation?docID=Genealo gy-glh20904590] (9/10/2004)

[81] King, Donald L. "Re: HTB - more info." E-mail to John Kossik. 7/13/2005.

[82] Anonymous, The Book of Detroiters : a biographical dictionary of leading living men of the city of Detroit Chicago: A.N. Marquis & Co., 1908, p. 85
[http://persi.heritagequestonline.com/hqoweb/library/do/books/results/image?ur

n=urn%3Aproquest%3AUS%3Bglhbooks%3BGenealogy-glh20904590%3B88%3B-1%3B&polarity=&scale=&jumptophysicalpage=85] (8/15/2004)

[83] 1900 US Census, **Series:** T623 **Roll:** 747 **Page:** 87,
[http://persi.heritagequestonline.com/hqoweb/library/do/census/results/image?s ur-name=giddings&series=12&state=9&countyid=673&hitcount=3&p=1&urn=urn%3Ap roquest%3AUS%3Bcensus%3B16990881%3B131726895%3B12%3B9&searchtype=1&off set=2] (9/2004)

[84] 1910 US Census, **Series:** T624 **Roll:** 110 **Page:** 4,
[http://persi.heritagequestonline.com/hqoweb/library/do/census/results/image?s ur-name=brush&givenname=frederick&series=13&state=16&hitcount=1&p=1&urn=urn %3Aproquest%3AUS%3Bcensus%3B4717611%3B32234892%3B13%3B16&searchtype= 1&offset=0] (9/2004)

[85] Ommen, L. "RE: Tulare County Historical Society Inquiry" E-mail to John Kossik. 5/11/2005.

[86] Colonel Allensworth State Historical Park, California State Parks, 2003,
[http://www.parks.ca.gov/pages/583/files/ColonelAllensworth.pdf] (6/2005)

[87] Ancestry.com. California Death Index, 1940-1997. [database online] Provo, UT:Ancestry.com, 2000. Original electronic data: State of California. California Death Index, 1940-1997. Sacramento, CA: State of California Department of Health Services, Center for Health Statistics, 19--.

[88] James A. Brush last appears in City Directories of Detroit in 1874, see:
Anonymous. J.W. Weeks & Co.'s annual directory of the inhabitants, business firms, incorporated companies, etc., of Detroit, for 1874-75.Detroit: J.W. Weeks & Co., 1874, p.169. [http://persi.heritagequestonline.com/] (7/2/2005)

[89] Brush, Bert. Self Portrait. Photo. The Museum of Snohomish County History. Everett WA

[90] Photographic Chemical Descriptions, SODIUM THIOSULFATE,
[http://www.jackspcs.com/chemdesc.htm] (7/14/2005)

[91] Article on biography on Bert J. Brush from The Museum of Snohomish County History, Everett WA.

[92] Taft, Del, grandson of Bert J. Brush, personal communication with John Kossik, 7/14/2005.

# Chapter 3

[1] Anonymous, Detroit blue book : a society directory for the city of Detroit, containing the names of several thousand householders and prominent citizens, also alphabetical directory of heads of families. Detroit, Mich.: Detroit Free Press Pub. Co., c1885, 391 pgs.
[http://persi.heritagequestonline.com/hqoweb/library/do/books/results/image/d ownload?urn=urn%3Aproquest%3AUS%3Bglhbooks%3BGenealogy-glh20906359%3B-1%3B-1%3B] (2/28/06)

[2] 1900 US Census, Michigan, County of Wayne, City of Detroit, 1st Ward, Sheet 6, 69 Alfred Street.

[3] Brunk, Dr. Thomas W.. "63 Alfred Street." E-mail to John Kossik. March 4, 2006.

[4] Brunk, Dr. Thomas W.. "63 Alfred amendment." E-mail to John Kossik. March 4, 2006.

[5] Wayne State University, College of Urban, Labor and Metropolitan Affairs, Aerial Photo Collection, City of Detroit 1961,
[http://techtools.culma.wayne.edu/media/wayne/1961/fm-30-127.pdf](2/28/05)

[6] Wayne State University, College of Urban, Labor and Metropolitan Affairs, Aerial Photo Collection, City of Detroit 1981, [http://techtools.culma.wayne.edu/media/wayne/1981/17562-15-418.pdf](2/28/05)

[7] Campbell Gibson, Population Of The 100 Largest Cities And Other Urban Places In The United States: 1790 To 1990. Population Division Working Paper No. 27. Population Division. U.S. Bureau of the Census. Washington, D.C. June 1998. [http://www.census.gov/population/www/documentation/twps0027.html] (10/17/06)

[8] Anonymous, Detroit city directory for 1882 : embracing an alphabetical list of business firms and private citizens, a directory of the city and county officers, churches, public and private schools, benevolent, literary and other associations, banks and incorporated institutions, and a complete classified business directory of Detroit, also a classified business directory of Windsor, Ont., J.W. Weeks & Co., Detroit, 1882 [http://persi.heritagequestonline.com.access-proxy.sno-isle.org/] (11/12/2006)

[9] Dau's Detroit Society Blue Book and Ladies' Address Book: Elite family Directory: Official Club Lists, Dau Publishing Company, Detroit, MI, 1902. [http://www.heritagequestonline.com/] (8/31/2004)

[10] Anonymous, Detroit blue book : a society directory for the city of Detroit, containing the names of several thousand householders and prominent citizens, also alphabetical directory of heads of families., Detroit Free Press Pub. Co., Detroit, Mich., 1885.

[11] Ibid

[12] Ibid

[13] Ibid

[14] Warranty Deed Charles Stinchfield to Alanson J. Fox, 1888

[15] 1880 US Census. Erwin, Steuben, New York. Page No. 213B [http://www.familysearch.org/End/search/Census/Household] (2/8/2006)

[16] Trowbridge, M.E.D. History of Baptists in Michigan. Michigan Baptist State Convention. 1909. P. 293. [http://persi.heritagequestonline.com/] (10/24/2006)

[17] Fox, William F. Daniel Fox of East Haddam, Ct. and some of his descendants. Fort Orange Press. Albany, NY. 1890. [http://persi.heritagequestonline.com/hqweb/library/do/books/] (10/25/2006)

[18] Smith, H.P., Ed. History of Warren County, D. Mason & Co., Syracuse, NY, 1885.

[19] Keesler, M.P., MOHAWK - Discovering the Valley of the Crystals, Chapter 9 - The Yankee Invasion, 2002, They Burned The Woods and Sold the Ashes, [http://www.paulkeeslerbooks.com/Potash.html](10/16/2006)

[20] Potash, Wikipedia, [http://en.wikipedia.org/wiki/Potash](10/16/2006)

[21] Ashery, Wikipedia, [http://en.wikipedia.org/wiki/Ashery](10/16/2006)

[22] First US Patent July 31, 1790 from US patent and Trademarks site [http://patft.uspto.gov/netacgi/nph-Parser?Sect1=PTO2&Sect2=HITOFF&u=%2Fnetahtml%2FPTO%2Fsearch-adv.htm&r=1&p=1&f=G&l=50&d=PALL&S1=1790$.PD.&OS=ISD/$/$/1790&RS=ISD/1790$$](11/7/2006)

[23] Smith, H.P., Ed. History of Warren County, D. Mason & Co., Syracuse, NY, 1885.

[24] Cutter, W.R., Genealogical and Family History of Western New York, Lewis Historical Publishing Company, New York, 1912.

[25] LeDuc, Vonciel, Manistique, MI, Personal communication with John Kossik, October 2006.

[26] Trowbridge, M.E.D., History of Baptists in Michigan, Michigan Baptist State Convention, 1909. [http://persi.heritagequestonline.com/](10/24/2006)

[27] Fox, William F. Daniel Fox of East Haddam, Ct. and some of his descendants. Fort Orange Press. Albany, NY. 1890. [http://persi.heritagequestonline.com/hqweb/library/do/books/] (10/25/2006)

[28] Trowbridge, M.E.D., History of Baptists in Michigan, Michigan Baptist State Convention, 1909. [http://persi.heritagequestonline.com/](10/24/2006)

[29] Fox, H., Fox family news, volumes 1-10 inclusive (1912-1921) : the official organ of the Society of the Descendants of Norman Fox, New York, 1925?, Fox Family news:

Vol IV. No. 4 July 1, 1915, pp. 19-21
[http://persi.heritagequestonline.com/](10/24/2006)
[30] Five Ways to Compute the Relative Value of a U.S. Dollar Amount, 1790 – 2005, MeasuringWorth.com, 2006,
[http://www.measuringworth.com/calculators/compare/result.php](11/7/2006)
[31] Fox, H., Fox family news, volumes 1-10 inclusive (1912-1921) : the official organ of the Society of the Descendants of Norman Fox, New York, 1925?, Fox Family news: Vol. V No. 1 January, 1916, pp. 2-3.
[http://persi.heritagequestonline.com/](10/24/2006)
[32] Fox, H., Fox family news, volumes 1-10 inclusive (1912-1921) : the official organ of the Society of the Descendants of Norman Fox, New York, 1925?, Fox Family news: Vol IV. No. 4 July 1, 1915, pp. 19-21
[http://persi.heritagequestonline.com/](10/24/2006)
[33] Battle of Harpers Ferry, Wikipedia,
[http://en.wikipedia.org/wiki/Battle_of_Harpers_Ferry](11/8/2006)
[34] Gilbert, David T., Guide to Harpers Ferry History, Harpers Ferry National Historical Park, Last Updated: Thursday, 02-Jun-2005 10:43:12 Eastern Daylight Time.
[http://www.nps.gov/archive/hafe/history.htm](1/30/2007)
[35] Fox, A.J., Letter to Uncle Robt. Painted Post October 15, 1862. Courtesy of Louise Barker, Family Archivist, Society of the Descendants of Norman Fox.
[36] Five Ways to Compute the Relative Value of a U.S. Dollar Amount, 1790 – 2005, MeasuringWorth.com, 2006,
[http://www.measuringworth.com/calculators/compare/result.php](11/8/2006)
[37] US Census 1870, Erwin, Steuben county, NY, Post Office Painted Post, p. 22.
[38] Great Chicago Fire, Wikipedia,
[http://en.wikipedia.org/wiki/Great_Chicago_Fire](11/8/2006)
[39] Various articles, LeDuc, Vonciel, Memories Columns, Pioneer-Tribune, Manistique, MI, June to December 2005.
[40] Ibid
[41] Ibid
[42] Obituary Publication Unknown, Alanson J. Fox is Dead, Nov. 1903. Courtesy of Louise Barker, Family Archivist, Society of the Descendants of Norman Fox.
[43] LeDuc, Vonciel, Manistique, MI, Personal communication with John Kossik, October 2006.
[44] Various articles, LeDuc, Vonciel, Memories Columns, Pioneer-Tribune, Manistique, MI, June to December 2005.
[45] Ashworth, W., The Late, Great Lakes: An Environmental History, Wayne State University Press, 1987, pp. 67-80. [http://books.google.com/books?id=qWKjS_yB-GoC] (12/4/08)
[46] Cutter, W.R., Genealogical and family history of western New York : a record of the achievements of her people in the making of a commonwealth and the building of a nation, Lewis Historical Publishing Co., New York, 1912, pp. 1017-1018.
[http://persi.heritagequestonline.com/](10/24/2006)
[47] Fox, William F. Daniel Fox of East Haddam, Ct. and some of his descendants. Fort Orange Press. Albany, NY. 1890.
[http://persi.heritagequestonline.com/hqweb/library/do/books/] (10/25/2006)
[48] Fox, H., Fox family news, volumes 1-10 inclusive (1912-1921) : the official organ of the Society of the Descendants of Norman Fox. New York: H. Fox, 1925, 273 pgs, Jan. 1, 1915, p. 2, Sept. 1, 1921, pp. 17-18 [http://persi.heritagequestonline.com.access-proxy.sno-isle.org] (10/24/2006 & 12/3/2008)
[49] Obituary Publication Unknown, Alanson J. Fox is Dead, Nov. 1903. Courtesy of Louise Barker, Family Archivist, Society of the Descendants of Norman Fox.
[50] Olsen, P. "Re: Alanson J. Fox" E-mail to John Kossik. September 6, 2006.
[51] Ivins D.D. & Freeman A.S., The Fox Genealogy: The ancestors and Descendants of Jehiel Fox (1762-1823) of Canaan, Hoosick Falls, and Chester, New York. 1903. Courtesy of Louise Barker, Family Archivist, Society of the Descendants of Norman Fox.

[52] Fox, A.J., Speech Taxation and Tariffs, Detroit Home and Day School, March 26, 1897, Courtesy of Louise Barker, Family Archivist, Society of the Descendants of Norman Fox.

[53] Ibid

[54] Edwards, Rebecca, The Currency Question: The Gold Standard, Bimetallism, or 'Free Silver'?, Vassar College, 2000.[ http://projects.vassar.edu/1896/currency.html] (1/23/2006).

[55] Fox, A.J., Speech Untitled, Late October 1896, Courtesy of Louise Barker, Family Archivist, Society of the Descendants of Norman Fox.

[56] Ibid

[57] Edwards, Rebecca, The Currency Question: The Gold Standard, Bimetallism, or 'Free Silver'?, Vassar College, 2000.[ http://projects.vassar.edu/1896/currency.html] (1/23/2006).

[58] Fox, A.J., Speech Memorial Day Address at Painted Post NY, May 30, 1889, Courtesy of Louise Barker, Family Archivist, Society of the Descendants of Norman Fox.

[59] Fox, A.J., Speech The Value of Early Investments, Remarks by A. J. Fox of Detroit before Baptist Home Mission Society at Saratoga Springs, May 30, 1895, Courtesy of Louise Barker, Family Archivist, Society of the Descendants of Norman Fox.

[60] Fox, A.J., Speech Taxation and Tariffs, Detroit Home and Day School, March 26, 1897, Courtesy of Louise Barker, Family Archivist, Society of the Descendants of Norman Fox.

[61] Fox, A.J., Speech Memorial Day Address at Painted Post NY, May 30, 1889, Courtesy of Louise Barker, Family Archivist, Society of the Descendants of Norman Fox.

[62] Fox, A.J., Speech The Value of Early Investments, Remarks by A. J. Fox of Detroit before Baptist Home Mission Society at Saratoga Springs, May 30, 1895, Courtesy of Louise Barker, Family Archivist, Society of the Descendants of Norman Fox.

[63] Brunk, Thomas W., "63 Alfred Street", E-mail to John Kossik, March 4, 2006.

[64] Pictures of the stable behind the Ransom Gillis House taken in the Fall of 1904, Courtesy of Thomas W. Brunk, Ph.D., Received March 2006 by John Kossik.

[65] 1900 US Census, State Michigan, County Wayne, City of Detroit, 1st Ward, Supervisors's District 116, Enumeration 6, Sheet 6.

[66] McLauchlin, Russell, Alfred Street, Conjure House, Detroit, 1946, p. 13

[67] Ibid, p. 95.

[68] Ibid, p. 102.

[69] Perry, Mary C., Excerpt from her autobiography-Chapter VII, "Pewabic Pottery." E-mail to John Kossik from Sandy Koukoulas. September 17, 2004.

[70] Perry, Mary C., Excerpt from her autobiography-Chapter VII, "Pewabic Pottery," pp. 33, 51.

[71] Fox, A.J., Last Will and Testament, October 1903.

[72] Gravestone of Alanson J. Fox, Woodmere Cemetery, Detroit, MI, Picture by John Kossik.

[73] Obituary Publication Unknown, Alanson J. Fox is Dead, Nov. 1903. Courtesy of Louise Barker, Family Archivist, Society of the Descendants of Norman Fox.

[74] Bacteremia, Wikipedia, [http://en.wikipedia.org/wiki/Blood_poisoning](11/12/2006)

[75] Society Page, Detroit New Tribune, Sunday October 16, 1904, 17:3, of 1904, Courtesy of Thomas W. Brunk, Ph.D., Received March 2006 by John Kossik.

[76] 1910 US Census, Series: T624 Roll: 679 Page: 130, State Michigan, County Wayne, City Detroit, Ward 1st, Enumeration District 11, sheets 6-7. [http://persi.heritagequestonline.com.access-proxy.sno-isle.org/] (11/15/2006)

[77] Dau's Detroit blue book and ladies' address book: elite family directory, official club lists, Dau Publishing Co., Detroit, Michigan, 1906 & 1908.

Dau's blue book for Detroit: including Ann Arbor, Birmingham, Grosse Ile, Grosse Pointe , Grosse Pointe Farms, Mt. Clemens, Northville, Pontiac, Orchard Lake, Wyandotte, Ypsilanti, Dau Publishing Co., New York, 1911.

Dau's blue book for Detroit and suburban towns, Dau Publishing Co., New York, 1914 & 1917. [http://www.heritagequestonline.com/] (8/31/2004)

[78] Warranty Deed between Cornelia S. Fox and Maurice Penfield Fikes, June 6, 1916.
[79] Blosser, J.A., Blosser Travelogues, 1914.
[http://sdrcdata.lib.uiowa.edu/libsdrc/details.jsp?id=/blosser/1] (11/15/2006)
[80] Ivins D.D. & Freeman A.S., The Fox Genealogy: The ancestors and Descendants of Jehiel Fox (1762-1823) of Canaan, Hoosick Falls, and Chester, New York. 1903. Courtesy of Louise Barker, Family Archivist, Society of the Descendants of Norman Fox.
[81] 1910 US Census, **Series:** T624 **Roll:** 679 **Page:** 130, State Michigan, County Wayne, City Detroit, Ward 1st, Enumeration District 11, sheets 6-7.
[http://persi.heritagequestonline.com.access-proxy.sno-isle.org/] (11/15/2006)

## Chapter 4

[1] Boyle, K., Getis, V., Muddy Boots and Ragged Aprons: Images of Working-Class Detroit, 1900-1930, Wayne State University Press, Detroit, 1997, p. 36.
[2] 1910 US Census, **Series:** T624 **Roll:** 681 **Page:** 2, State Michigan, County Wayne, City Detroit, Ward 4th, Enumeration District 47, sheet 2.
[http://persi.heritagequestonline.com.acess-proxy.sno-isle.org/] (11/17/2006)
[3] 1900 US Census, **Series:** T623 **Roll:** 752 **Page:** 105, State Michigan, County Wayne, City Detroit, Ward 13th, Enumeration District 148, sheet 15.
[http://persi.heritagequestonline.com.acess-proxy.sno-isle.org/] (11/17/2006)
[4] Warranty Deed, Maurice Penfield Fikes to Bertha Noeske et al., July 22, 1919.
[5] 1920 US Census, **Series:** T625 **Roll:** 802 **Page:** 36, State Michigan, County Wayne, City Detroit, Ward 1st, Enumeration District 13, sheet 10.
[http://persi.heritagequestonline.com.acess-proxy.sno-isle.org/] (11/17/2006)
[6] Sanborn Maps, Detroit, Michigan, Volume 3, 1921, Sheet 1, 2001
[http://sanborn.umi.com/mi/3985/dateid-000010.htm] (11/17/2006).
[7] 1920 US Census, State Michigan, County Wayne, City Detroit, Ward 1st, Enumeration District 22, sheet 9. [http://persi.heritagequestonline.com.acess-proxy.sno-isle.org/] (11/17/2006)
[8] Boyle, K., Getis, V., Muddy Boots and Ragged Aprons: Images of Working-Class Detroit, 1900-1930, Wayne State University Press, Detroit, 1997, pp. 62-73.
[9] Ibid, p. 68.
[10] Conot, Robert, American Odyssey, Wayne State University Press, Detroit, 1986, pp. 132-139.
[11] Anonymous, The Detroit society address book : elite family directory, club membership, 1900-1901., Dau Pub. Co., New York, 1900.
[http://persi.heritagequestonline.com.access-proxy.sno-isle.org/] (11/19/2006)
[12] Anonymous, Dau's blue book for Detroit: including Ann Arbor, Birmingham, Grosse Ile, Grosse Pointe, Grosse Pointe Farms, Mt. Clemens, Northville, Pontiac, Orchard Lake, Wyandotte, Ypsilanti, Dau Pub. Co., New York, 1911.
[http://www.heritagequestonline.com] (8/31/2004)
[13] Dau's blue book for Detroit and suburban towns, Dau's Blue Books, Inc., New York, 1917. [http://persi.heritagequestonline.com.access-proxy.sno-isle.org/] (8/31/2004).
[14] Old and New House Numbers 1920-1921 Detroit, Wayne Co., Michigan,
[http://mipolonia.net/old_new_addys/old_new_addys.htm] (12/03/2006).
[15] Sanborn Maps, Alfred Street Detroit, 1921 (need to add more detail, properly document this endnote)
[16] Brunk, Dr. Thomas W., Re: 63 Alfred amendment, E-mail to John Kossik, March 7, 2006.
[17] City of Detroit Real Property Inquiry System Property Data & Long Legal Descriptions, 2832 John R, Brush Sub of Pt of Pk Lots 12 & 13 (Plats),
[http://www4.ci.detroit.mi.us/CityofDetroit](3/1/2005)
[18] Sheriff's Deed on Mortgage Sale, 9/25/1936.
[19] 1920 US Census, State Michigan, County Wayne, City Detroit, Ward 1st, Enumeration District 22, sheet 9. [http://persi.heritagequestonline.com.acess-proxy.sno-isle.org/] (11/17/2006)

[20] 1930 US Census, State Michigan, County Wayne, City Detroit, Ward 1st, Enumeration District 82-9, sheets 15B-16B. [http://persi.heritagequestonline.com.acessproxy.sno-isle.org/] (11/17/2006)

## Chapter 5

[1] Creelman, James, The Slaughter of Christians in Asia Minor, The New York Times, August 22, 1909
[2] Ibid.
[3] Essa, Peter, Personal Communication with John Kossik, March 23, 2007.
[4] Binno, Pete, Re: Massacre in Adana, Turkey, e-mail to John Kossik, April 9, 2007.
[5] Armenian Wealth Caused Massacres, The New York Times, April 25, 1909.
[6] Abdul Hamid II, Wikipedia [http://en.wikipedia.org/wiki/Abdülhamid_II] (4/18/2007)
[7] Islam vs. Liberalism, The New York Times, April 15. 1909.
[8] Halsall, Paul, Modern History Sourcebook: The Young Turks: Proclamation for the Ottoman Empire, 1908, June 1998 [http://www.fordham.edu/halsall/mod/1908youngturk.html] (4/18/2007)
[9] Facing History and Ourselves Foundation, Inc., Humanity Crimes Against Humanity and Civilization: The Genocide of the Armenians, Facing History and Ourselves, Brookline, MA, 2004, pp. 51-71.
[10] Armenia, Wikipedia [http://en.wikipedia.org/wiki/Armenia] (4/18/2007)
[11] Foreign Cruisers at Mersina, The New York Times, April 23, 1909.
[12] Days of Horror Described: American Missionary and Eyewitness of Murder and Rapine, The New York Times, April 28, 1909.
[13] Brooklyn Man Saw Missionaries Shot, The New York Times, May 2, 1909.
[14] Creelman, James, The Red Terror on the Cilician Plain, The New York Times, August 29, 1909.
[15] Facing History and Ourselves Foundation, Inc., Humanity Crimes Against Humanity and Civilization: The Genocide of the Armenians, Facing History and Ourselves, Brookline, MA, 2004, pp. 51-71
[16] Ibid
[17] Islam vs. Liberalism, The New York Times, April 15, 1909.
[18] Armenian Wealth Caused Massacres, The New York Times, April 25, 1909.
[19] American Women in Peril at Hadjin, The New York Times, April 23, 1909.
[20] THE ARMENIANS in the Late Ottoman Period, The Turkish Historical Society for The Council Of Culture, Arts And Publications Of The Grand National Assembly Of Turkey, Ankara, 2001, pp. 51-53. [http://www.tbmm.gov.tr/yayinlar/yayin1/armenian.htm] (04/17/2007).
[21] Creelman, James, The Slaughter of Christians in Asia Minor, The New York Times, August 22, 1909.
[22] Essa, Peter, Personal Communication with John Kossik, February 16, 2007.
[23] Jammo, Sarhad, Contemporary Chaldeans and Assyrians Primordial Nation, One Original Church, St. Peter The Apostle Catholic Diocese for Chaldeans and Assyrians USA, 2002-2006. [http://www.kaldu.org/3_chaldean_culture/ContemporaryChaldeansAssyrians.html] (4/18/2007)
[24] Binno, Pete, Re: Massacre in Adana, Turkey, e-mail to John Kossik, April 9, 2007.
[25] Tel Keppe, Wikipedia, [http://en.wikipedia.org/wiki/Tel_Keppe] (4/23/2007)
[26] Essa, Peter, Personal Communication with John Kossik, March 19, 2007.
[27] Essa, Peter, Personal Communication with John Kossik, February 23, 2007.
[28] Syrian Desert, Wikipedia, [http://en.wikipedia.org/wiki/Syrian_Desert] (4/23/2007)
[29] Palmyra, Wikipedia, [http://en.wikipedia.org/wiki/Tadmur] (4/24/2007)
[30] Year: 1930; Census Place: Detroit, Wayne, Michigan; Roll: 1044; Page: 8A; Enumeration District: 317; Image: 341.0.

[31] Year: 1930; Census Place: Detroit, Wayne, Michigan; Roll: 1044; Page: 8A; Enumeration District: 319; Image: 382.0.

[32] Essa, Peter, Personal Communication with John Kossik, March 23, 2007.

[33] Essa, Peter, Personal Communication with John Kossik.

[34] Lambe, Kristy, Getting the Ducks out of the Bathtub: The Hygiene and Americanization Campaigns of the Ford Sociological Department, 1914-1921, Undergraduate History Honors Thesis, University of Michigan, March 31, 2004

[35] Boyle, K., Getis, V., Muddy Boots and Ragged Aprons: Images of Working-Class Detroit, 1900-1930, Wayne State University Press, Detroit, 1997.

[36] Conot, Robert, American Odyssey, Wayne State University Press, Detroit, 1986, pp. 163-165.

[37] Essa, Peter, Personal Communication with John Kossik, February 23, 2007.

[38] Essa, Peter, Personal Communication with John Kossik, March 23, 2007.

[39] Binno, Pete, Emailing: Copy of Saint Maron's Church Photograph, e-mail to John Kossik, April 2, 2007.

[40] U.S. Census Bureau, Census 2000 Summary File 3, Matrices PCT15 and PCT18. [http://factfinder.census.gov/servlet/QTTable?-geo_id=04000US26&-qr_name=DEC_2000_SF3_U_QTP13&-ds_name=DEC_2000_SF3_U] (4/25/2007)

[41] Essa, Peter, Personal Communication with John Kossik, March 23, 2007.

[42] Albert Nelson Marquis, ed. The Book of Detroiters, 1908, A.N. Marquis & Company, Chicago, p. 188.

[43] Anonymous, Dau's Detroit blue book and ladies' address book : elite family directory, official club lists. Detroit, Mich.: Dau Pub. Co., 1907, p.55.

[44] Year: 1930; Census Place: Detroit, Wayne, Michigan; Roll: 1044; Page 8A; Enumeration District: 317; Image: 341.0.

[45] Year: 1930; Census Place: Detroit, Wayne, Michigan; Page 15A; Enumeration District: 82-9.

[46] Sheriff's Deed on Mortgage Sale, Fred A. Bell, Deputy Sheriff Wayne County & The Detroit Bank, 25-September-1936.

[47] Binno, Pete, Personal Conversation with John Kossik, February 2007.

[48] Kossik, John, Photo of Ransom Gillis House, 2/11/2005.

[49] "Picture of Ransom Gillis Home." Burton Historical Collection, Detroit Public Library, Detroit, MI.

[50] Essa, Peter, Personal Communication with John Kossik, March 23, 2007.

[51] Essa, Peter, Personal Communication with John Kossik, September 2008.

[52] McLauchlin, Russell. Alfred Street. Detroit: Conjure House, 1946.

[53] McLauchlin, Russell, Town Talk, The Detroit News, August 28, 1944.

[54] City of Detroit, Real Property Inquiry System, Property Data & Long Legal Descriptions, 2832 John R, [http://www4.ci.detroit.mi.us/CityofDetroit/] (3/1/2005)

[55] Gavrilovich, P., McGraw, B. Ed., The Detroit Almanac: 300 years of life in the Motor City, Detroit Free Press, Detroit, 2001, p. 108.

[56] Essa, Peter, Personal Communication with John Kossik, March 19, 2007.

[57] Deed of sale between The Detroit Bank & John J. Essa and Amina Essa, 20-May-1942.

[58] Conot, Robert, American Odyssey, Wayne State University Press, Detroit, 1986, Chapter 81

[59] Gavrilovich, P., McGraw, B. Ed., The Detroit Almanac: 300 years of life in the Motor City, Detroit Free Press, Detroit, 2001, p. 108.

[60] Sugrue, Thomas J., The Origins of the Urban Crisis: Race and Inequality in Postwar Detroit, Princeton University Press, Princeton & Oxford, 2005, Chapter 2.

[61] Says Black Legion Murdered a Negro, New York Times, July 22, 1936.

[62] Seven 'Vigilantes' Accused of Murder, New York Times, May 23, 1936.

[63] Housing Crisis Hits Detroit War Zone, New York Times, March 31, 1942.

[64] Sugrue, Thomas J., The Origins of the Urban Crisis: Race and Inequality in Postwar Detroit, Princeton University Press, Princeton & Oxford, 2005, p. 74.

[65] Detroiters in Riot on Negro Project, New York Times, March 1, 1942.

[66] Ibid
[67] 800 Soldiers Protect 12 Families Moving In, New York Times, April 30, 1942.
[68] Baulch, V.M. and Zacharias, P., The 1943 Detroit race riots, The Detroit News, [http://info.detnews.com/history/story/index.cfm?id=185&category=events] (05/04/2007)
[69] United Press, Injured Reach 600, New York Times, June 22, 1943.
[70] Army Patrols End Detroit Rioting; Death Toll at 29, New York Times, June 23,1943.
[71] Baulch, V.M. and Zacharias, P., The 1943 Detroit race riots, The Detroit News, [http://info.detnews.com/history/story/index.cfm?id=185&category=events] (05/04/2007)
[72] Gavrilovich, P., McGraw, B. Ed., The Detroit Almanac: 300 years of life in the Motor City, Detroit Free Press, Detroit, 2001, p. 108.
[73] Sugrue, Thomas J., The Origins of the Urban Crisis: Race and Inequality in Postwar Detroit, Princeton University Press, Princeton & Oxford, 2005, pp. 209-229.
[74] Ibid, p. 214.
[75] Army Patrols End Detroit Rioting; Death Toll at 29, New York Times, June 23,1943.
[76] Many Negroes Buy 'White' Residences, New York Times, January 22, 1961.
[77] Ibid.
[78] Michigan Pushes Realty Bias Rule, New York Times, June 10, 1962.
[79] Realty Brokers See Themselves Beset by New Anti-Bias Laws, New York Times, November 18, 1962.
[80] Sugrue, Thomas J., The Origins of the Urban Crisis: Race and Inequality in Postwar Detroit, Princeton University Press, Princeton & Oxford, 2005, pp. 195-196.
[81] Detroit Negroes Push School Issue, New York Times, June 2, 1963.
[82] Essa, Peter, Personal Communication with John Kossik, March 19, 2007.
[83] Quit Claim Deed, 205 Alfred Street, Detroit, MI, January 9, 1973.

## Chapter 6

[1] Woodward East Project, Inc., Report, Recreation Needs, 1969.
[2] Schramm, J.E., Henning, W.H., "When Eastern Michigan Rode the Rails II: THE RAPID RAILWAY and Detroit-Port Huron BY RAIL-SHIP-BUS", Interurban Press, Glendale, 1986.
[3] O'Toole, R. A Desire Named Streetcar How Federal Subsidies Encourage Wasteful Local Transit Systems, Cato Institute, Policy Analysis no. 559, January 5, 2006, [http://www.cato.org/pubs/pas/pa559.pdf] (1/31/2010)
[4] Wikipedia contributors, 'Detroit', Wikipedia, The Free Encyclopedia, [http://en.wikipedia.org/w/index.php?title=Detroit&oldid=341217743] (2/1/ 2010)
[5] Sugrue, Thomas J., The Origins of the Urban Crisis: Race and Inequality in Postwar Detroit, Princeton University Press, Princeton & Oxford, 2005, pp. 20-21.
[6] Schramm,"When Eastern Michigan Rode the Rails II: THE RAPID RAILWAY and Detroit-Port Huron BY RAIL-SHIP-BUS"
[7] Goodspeed, R.C., Urban Renewal In Postwar Detroit: The Gratiot Area Redevelopment Project: A Case Study, 2004 History Honors Thesis, The University of Michigan, Adviser: Prof. Stephen Ward.
[8] Lukas, A.J., "Whitey Hasn't Got The Message,' New Your Times (1923-Current file); Aug 27, 1967; ProQUest Historical Newspapers The New Your Times (1851-2006), p. SM113.
[9] Ibid.
[10] Ibid.
[11] 'Milliken v. Bradley/Dissent Marshall', Wikisource, The Free Library, [http://en.wikisource.org/w/index.php?title=Milliken_v._Bradley/Dissent_Marshall &oldid=638698] (2/3/2010)
[12] 'Milliken v. Bradley', Wikisource, The Free Library, [http://en.wikisource.org/w/index.php?title=Milliken_v._Bradley&oldid=638695] (2/3/2010)

[13] Riddle, D., Race and Reaction in Warren, Michigan, 1971 to 1974: Bradley V. Milliken and the Cross-District Busing Controversy, Michigan Historical Review, Vol. 26, 2000,
[http://www.questia.com/googleScholar.qst;jsessionid=LpKfVyd0m6wTxlLMphp2N 3by6lvvtqXvbP2kJCQvvNtJYMnZccLR!1680139891!2144018255?docId=5002380945] (2/2/2010)
[14] Wikipedia contributors, 'Detroit', Wikipedia, The Free Encyclopedia,
[http://en.wikipedia.org/w/index.php?title=Detroit&oldid=341520676] (2/3/2010)
[15] Erntcq, J.M., URBAN RENEWAL HISTORY OF DETROIT 1946-1970, International Urban Studies, Center for Urban Studies, Wayne State University, Detroit, Michigan, March, 1972.
[16] Fairman, J., Citizens force cleanup, It's a fight for survival, Woodward East neighbors unite, The Detroit News, July 11, 1969, p. 20-D.
[17] Woodward East Project, Inc., Report, Recreation Needs, 1969.
[18] Ibid.
[19] Ward, H. H., Woodward East Project: People's Group to Launch 7 Houses, Hotel for Poor, Detroit Free Press, Unknown date probably 1969, Walter P. Reuther Library, Wayne State University.
[20] Fairman, J., Citizens force cleanup, It's a fight for survival, Woodward East neighbors unite, The Detroit News, July 11, 1969, p. 20-D.
[21] Meeting Minutes, 11/21/1968, Woodward East Project, Walter P. Reuther Library, Wayne State University.
[22] Meeting Minutes, 4/24/1969, Woodward East Project, Walter P. Reuther Library, Wayne State University.
[23] Ward, H. H., Woodward East Project: People's Group to Launch 7 Houses, Hotel for Poor, Detroit Free Press, Unknown date probably 1969, Walter P. Reuther Library, Wayne State University.
[24] Meeting Minutes, 11/17/1968, Woodward East Project, Walter P. Reuther Library, Wayne State University.
[25] Meeting Minutes, 8/10/1969, Woodward East Project, Walter P. Reuther Library, Wayne State University.
[26] The Sanborn Map Company, Sanborn Library LLC,
[http://sanborn.umi.com...Detroit+1910-1950+vol.+3%2C+1921%2C+Sheet+16.pdf],
[http://sanborn.umi.com...Detroit+1897+vol.+3%2C+Sheet+14.pdf] (8/30/2004)
[27] Meeting Minutes, 3/13/1969, Woodward East Project, Walter P. Reuther Library, Wayne State University.
[28] Brogan, M., Judge ends receivership for burned-put apartment, Detroit News, June 1969?, Walter P. Reuther Library, Wayne State University.
[29] Meeting Minutes, 6/18/1970, Woodward East Project, Walter P. Reuther Library, Wayne State University.
[30] Meeting Minutes, 2/13/1969, Woodward East Project, Walter P. Reuther Library, Wayne State University.
[31] Ibid.
[32] Quit Claim Deed, 205 Alfred Street, Detroit, MI, January 9, 1973.
[33] Meeting Minutes, 3/3/1969, Woodward East Project, Walter P. Reuther Library, Wayne State University.
[34] Meeting Minutes, 3/13/1969, Woodward East Project, Walter P. Reuther Library, Wayne State University.
[35] Meeting Minutes, 3/27/1969, Woodward East Project, Walter P. Reuther Library, Wayne State University.
[36] Meeting Minutes, 8/21/1969, Woodward East Project, Walter P. Reuther Library, Wayne State University.
[37] Meeting Minutes, 10/2/1969, Woodward East Project, Walter P. Reuther Library, Wayne State University.
[38] Internal correspondence of Lawrence Institute of Technology, From: Betty-lee Francis, Instructor, Preservation Architecture, School of Architecture, Lawrence Institute of

Technology, To: Architectural Preservation Students, July 7, 1975, from the personal files of John Merkler, received March 15, 2009.

[39] Barnett, J., 37 Design & Environment Projects - First Annual Review, 37 Design & Environment Projects - First Annual Review, Washington DC, 1976, pp. 54-55.

[40] Barnett, J., 37 Design & Environment Projects

[41] Personal conversation, John Kossik & Mike Kirk, 12/6/2005.

[42] Ibid.

[43] Photo of Ransom Gillis House, Bruce Harkness, 1977.

[44] Myers, P. Binder, G., Thinking Small: Transportation's Role in Neighborhood Revitalization: A Report on a Conference Held, February 22-24, 1978, Baltimore, Maryland, U.S. DEPARTMENT OF TRANSPORTATION, URBAN MASS TRANSPORTATION ADMINISTRATION, May 1979.

[45] Robinson v. Michigan Consol. Gas Co., United States Court of Appeals for the Sixth Circuit, 918 F.2d 579, November 1, 1990 [http://altlaw.org/v1/cases/499679] (11/6/08)

[46] Michigan.gov, Department of Energy, Labor,& Economic Growth, Corporate Entity Details, WOODWARD EAST PROJECT, INC

[47] Deed to the State of Michigan, G233968, LI19880, PA425, 6/3/1977.

[48] Deed under Act 223, Public Acts of 1909, as amended, G651769, LI21363, PA507, 3/18/1982.

[49] Powers, R., Urban pioneers, Michigan: The Magazine of the Detroit News, February 26, 1984, pp. 10-18.

[50] Ibid p. 16.

[51] Ibid p. 16.

[52] Barron, J., The Evangelist of Alfred Street, Monthly Detroit, October 1985, p. 87.

[53] Powers, R., Urban pioneers, p. 18.

[54] Powers, R., Urban pioneers, p. 16.

[55] Personal communication, February 4, 2010.

[56] Barron, J., The Evangelist of Alfred Street, p. 84.

[57] Photo of Ransom Gillis House, Bruce Harkness, 1977.

[58] Delores Bennett has been an activist for children and the poor in Detroit for decades. She is the founder of North End Youth Improvement Council. She served two terms as a member of the Wayne County Board of Commissioners being first elected in 1978. About the founder, North End Youth Improvement Council Web Site, [http://www.neyic.org/aboutthefounder.asp](2/5/2010).

[59] Photo, Courtesy of Scott Weir taken approx. 1984, personal communication Scott Weir to John Kossik Nov 21, 2005.

[60] Beverly Hills Cop, Paramount Pictures, December 5, 1984.

[61] Quit Claim Deed, Land in the City of Detroit, County of Wayne and State of Michigan being Lots 10 and 11, Block 6, Brush Subdivision of part of Park Lots 12 & 13 and part of Brush Farm adjoining. Red'd L. 1, P. 286 Plats, W.C.R., 13th day of November A.D. 1985.

[62] Personal conversation with Douglas Kuykendall, 6/30/2005.

[63] Personal conversation with Douglas Kuykendall, 10/24/2006.

[64] Ibid.

[65] Ibid.

[66] Personal conversation with Douglas Kuykendall, 6/30/2005.

[67] Photo, Ransom Gillis House, John Kossik, July 2004.

[68] Josar, D., How not to Rebuild Detroit, The Detroit News, 9/26/2005, [http://www.detnews.com/2005/metro/0509/27/A01-327216.htm?searchtext=Monday%2C+September+26%2C+2005] (07/06/2006)

[69] Personal conversation with Douglas Kuykendall, 10/24/2006.

[70] Ibid.

[71] Email, Kristine Kidorf to John Kossik, RE:Ransom Gillis Home, 8/19/2004.

[72] Powers, R., Urban pioneers, p. 16.

[73] Judgment, State of Michigan, in the Circuit Court for the County of Wayne, 01-125588-CC, 7/26/2001, JDG: Robert J Colombo, Detroit City of vs Woodward East

Project Inc., Parcel No. 229, Amended and Corrected Consent Judgment, May 6, 2004, Robert J. Colombo, Jr.
[74] Josar, D., How not to Rebuild Detroit.
[75] Personal conversation with Douglas Kuykendall, 10/24/2006.
[76] Mullen, A., Brush Park and hope: Old troubles and bold dreams as neighborhood charts a comeback, Metro Times, 1/2/2001,
[http://www.metrotimes.com/editorial/story.asp?id=1141] (2/8/2010)
[77] Josar, D., How not to Rebuild Detroit.
[78] Woodward Place at Brush Park, Conceptual Site Plan,
[http://www.crosswindsus.com/michigan/detroit_woodward_place/] (2/8/2010)
[79] Personal observations, John Kossik, July 2005 & February 2005.
[80] Email, Randy Wilcox to John Kossik, Re: Inside the Ransom Gillis Home, 9/8/2005.
[81] Email, Randy Wilcox to John Kossik, Re: Inside the Ransom Gillis Home, 9/11/2005.
[82] Personal communication, Brian V. Hurttienne, February 10, 2006.
[83] Email, Randy Wilcox to John Kossik, Re: Inside the Ransom Gillis Home, 9/11/2005.
[84] Email, Randy Wilcox to John Kossik, Re: Ransom Gillis images, 9/12/2005.
[85] Email, James Maurice to John Kossik, Re: 63 Alfred Street: Nowhere Else to Go, Online Book, 1/21/2009.
[86] Ibid.
[87] Pictures of Ransom Gillis House, Randy Wilcox, 1/15/2006 & 3/1/2006.
[88] dETROITfUNK: Ransom Roof,
[http://www.detroitfunk.com/2005/10/27/ransom_roof.htm] (06/08/2007).
[89] Personal Conversation, Peter Essa & John Kossik, 10/2008.
[90] Pictures of Ransom Gillis House, Randy Wilcox, 1/15/2006 & 3/1/2006.
[91] Email, James Marusich to John Kossik, Re: 63 Alfred Street: Nowhere Else to Go, Online Book, 1/20/2009.
[92] Email, James Marusich to John Kossik, Re: 63 Alfred Street: Nowhere Else to Go, Online Book, 1/21/2009.
[93] The Omega Man, Warner Bros., August 1, 1971 (U.S. release), Based on the novel "I Am Legend" by Richard Matheson also adapted for the film The Last Man on Earth in 1964 and I Am Legend in 2007.

## Chapter 7

[1] Rashid, Frank, Personal conversation with John Kossik, 10/3/2006.
[2] Cecil, A., 100-year-old time capsule opened in Detroit, Kalamazoo Gazette, January 2, 2001, page D6,
[http://blog.mlive.com/pagesofourpast/2008/11/oncall_request_time_capsule.html] (2/9/2010)
[3] John M. Donaldson, Rise of Architecture in Detroit, Century Box Letters, Detroit Century Box, Detroit Historical Museums & Society,
[http://www.detroithistorical.org/exhibits/index.asp?MID=3&EID=186&ID=204] (10/19/2005).
[4] WILLIAMS, C., Red Foxes Moving to Downtown Detroit Red foxes, other wildlife moving in to parts of Motor City abandoned by people, July 18, 2009, Associated Press,
[http://abcnews.go.com/US/wirestory?id=8118972&page=1] (2/9/2010).
[5] Harlow, P., Detroit: Too broke to bury their dead, October 1, 2009, CNNMoney.com,
[http://money.cnn.com/2009/10/01/news/economy/_morgue/index.htm] (2/9/2010).
[6] Rashid, Frank, Personal conversation with John Kossik, 10/3/2006.
[7] Okrent, D., Detroit: The Death — and Possible Life — of a Great City, Sep. 24, 2009, Time, [http://www.time.com/time/printout/0,8816,1925796,00.html] (9/29/2009)

[8] Carty, S.S., Labor talks may tiptoe around jobs bank, USA Today, 7/27/2007, [http://www.usatoday.com/money/autos/2007-07-23-uaw-talks-jobs-bank_N.htm] (2/10/2010)

[9] Gold J., Cuttin Worker Costs Key to Automakers' Survival, NPR, 12/23/2008, [http://www.npr.org/templates/story/story.php?storyId=98643230] (2/10/2010).

[10] Zywicki, T., Zywicki Comments on Automakers' Jobs Bank Program, Current News, George Mason University, School of Law, 11/26/2008 [http://www.law.gmu.edu/news/2008/5319] (2/10/2010).

[11] Tax Rates and Tax Burdens in the District of Columbia - A Nationwide Comparison 2007, Government of the District of Columbia, August 2008, [http://cfo.dc.gov/cfo/frames.asp?doc=/cfo/lib/cfo/07study-final.pdf](2/11/2010). It should be noted that yearly studies issued from the Government of the District of Columbia show variations in these rankings but Detroit consistently falls into the upper 10 to 15 in tax burdens while Seattle is consistently in the lower portion of this scale. The reader can explore these various data points by visiting the Government of the District of Columbia web site.

[12] Census 2000 Demographic Profile Highlights, Trenton city, Michigan, [http://factfinder.census.gov/servlet/SAFFFacts?_event=Search&geo_id=01000US&_geoContext=&_street=&_county=trenton&_cityTown=trenton&_state=04000US26&_zip=&_lang=en&_sse=on&ActiveGeoDiv=geoSelect&_useEV=&pctxt=fph&pgsl=010&_submenuId=factsheet_1&ds_name=ACS_2008_3YR_SAFF&_ci_nbr=null&qr_name=null&reg=null%3Anull&_keyword=&_industry=&show_2003_tab=&redirect=Y] (2/11/2010).

[13] CODE OF ORDINANCES CITY OF TRENTON, MICHIGAN, Published by Order of the City Council, Published by Municipal Code Corporation, Tallahassee, Florida 2004, OFFICIALS of the CITY OF TRENTON, MICHIGAN AT THE TIME OF THIS RECODIFICATION, CODE OF ORDINANCES, City of, TRENTON, MICHIGAN, Codified through Ord. No. 705-1, enacted Sept. 21, 2009. (Supplement No. 11), DIVISION 4. VACANT PROPERTY REGISTRATION AND MAINTENANCE, Sec. 18-200, (Ord. No. 720, § 1, 6-1-2009). [http://library1.municode.com/default-test/home.htm?infobase=13834&doc_action=whatsnew] (2/11/2010).

[14] Ibid.

[15] Ibid.

[16] Ibid.

[17] Ibid.

[18] Hall, C., Rolling out rain barrels saves water — and cash: But Detroit water department says thrifty devices force it to hike rates, Detroit Free Press, 8/22/2010,[ http://74.125.95.132/search?q=cache:cKRJlgy9woEJ:www.freep.com/apps/pbcs.dll/article?AID=/20090822/NEWS05/908220357&template=printart Detroit Water and Sewerage Department says the increasing use of water- saving devices such as rain barrels contributes to rate hikes], (10/22/09).

[19] French, R., Wilkinson, M., Leaving Michigan Behind: Eight-year population exodus staggers state: Outflow of skilled, educated workers crimps Michigan's recovery, April 02. 2009, The Detroit News, [http://detnews.com/article/20090402/METRO/904020403/Leaving-Michigan-Behind--Eight-year-population-exodus-staggers-state] (2/9/2010).

[20] French, R., Half of university grads flee Michigan State tries to bolster grad rates, but growing number move away, April 03. 2009, The Detroit News, [http://detnews.com/article/20090403/METRO/904030378#] (2/11/2010).

Made in the USA
Lexington, KY
05 March 2011